D1119122

When Your Heart Breaks,

It's Opening to Love

Healing and finding love after an affair, heartbreak or divorce

JOEY GARCIA

For Allison
May love
light your
way.
♡ Joey

Bodhisattva Publishers

Copyright © 2014 Joey Garcia

ALL RIGHTS RESERVED

Bodhisattva Publishers
P.O. Box 19841
Sacramento, CA 95819

ISBN 978-0-9889724-0-7

Library of Congress Control Number: 2013918775

FIRST EDITION

Cover image: Hope Harris (www.hopeimages.com)
Book design: Laura Martin

Contents

Introduction

"A broken heart is an open heart." – Joey Garcia

Once upon a time, a friend set me up on a blind date with a man she had known for over 20 years. When he called, I felt an immediate connection. On our first date, we lingered over our meal at a Mediterranean restaurant, discussing art, politics, religion and why our previous relationships had failed. He told me about his two children and his hopes for the future. On my porch, he hugged me long enough to let me know he was interested. I could feel him respectfully holding back from kissing me goodnight. Instead, he stepped back, looked directly into my eyes, smiled and said he wanted to see me again.

That night, I fell asleep happy about the possibility of a wonderful man in my life. He seemed to be everything I was looking for: intelligent, sophisticated, stable, playful, spiritual, well-traveled, well-groomed, respectful, and more. After his divorce he had even gone to therapy to clear the residue from his past and prepare himself to meet a new partner. I was charmed, curious and very attracted.

The next morning he called to say, "I just needed to hear your voice and be certain that our date last night was not a dream. When can I see you again?" It was as romantic as a fairytale; a fairytale I wanted to be true.

We dated for nearly a year. When I found out that he had cheated on his ex-wife, I didn't run. That was in the past, I thought. After all, he had gone to therapy and realized he had the affair because he wanted to end his marriage but lacked the courage to admit it to his wife or to his parents. His father was a pastor and his mother was the backbone of their church. They were very focused on appearances and had forced him to marry when he got his college girlfriend pregnant. He knew that the exit affair was immature and felt he had grown past it. After nine months or so, he told me that he loved our relationship and asked me to move in with him and his children. I loved his kids and we got along superbly. But I refused the invitation. When I did, he talked about marriage.

His adultery was a red flag, but I was too inexperienced in relationships to understand that at the time. I missed other red flags, too. His parents disliked me because I practiced a different religion than they did. They urged my boyfriend to get back together with his ex-girlfriend who shared their faith. When I caught him staring at women, not in the normal way of noticing an attractive person, but almost desperate to have that woman's eyes spotlighting him, I was floored. I requested that he stop. He couldn't. Eventually, he told me that before we began dating, he had an affair with a married woman at his gym. I wondered how many other liaisons he had engaged in before we met. I wondered how long it would be before it happened again.

We argued. I made demands. He made compromises. I knew it wouldn't work but found it difficult to leave. I clung to the dream birthed on our first date: the dream of a perfect match.

Finally, tired of my complaints about his lack of boundaries with women (which he claimed he learned by watching his father, the pastor), he broke up with me. He had met someone else and was giddily infatuated with her.

I was heartbroken. I didn't understand why he wouldn't change his behavior. The breakup activated other losses in my life, particularly the absence of support from my parents while I was growing up. The wound from my broken heart was deep and unrelenting. At times, I did not think I could carry on. I missed our Sunday suppers, our shared affection for foreign films, our conversations about the mundane and the essential, the perfect fit of our bodies, our weekends with the kids. And, even though he broke up with me, he wouldn't let go. Yes, he was dating someone else, but he still wanted me. I refused to see him, but I did accept two phone calls. On the second call, I thought back to his first marriage and figured it out.

"Do you still want to marry me?" I asked.

"I think about it," he said.

"Would you want to get married and still see other women?"

"Would you do that?"

"Please listen, very carefully. Don't ever call me again and don't contact me in any way. I wish you the best, but it's time for us to part."

I hung up, startled. What kind of nightmare had I led myself into? Had my craving for a relationship grown so out of control that I would accept a man who was incapable of the essential qualities of relationship? He was not trustworthy. He was not faithful. He was not able to sustain a commitment. We had chemistry and certain qualities of a friendship, but that is not enough to maintain a relationship long-term. Finally, gratitude sank in; I had saved myself from the sorrow his wife had endured. Plus, I had learned a lot about myself. I could identify various wounded places in myself that drew me into an unhealthy relationship, and I could see how to heal each one.

Much of what I learned I now offer to you in this book. Within these pages is the perspective that there is a deeper spiritual meaning within every dating relationship or marriage and its end. To gather all of the wisdom life generously offers, we must reflect on our choices with compassion and curiosity. We must also engage the effort necessary to change and welcome all of the ways love enters our lives. Most of all, we must be open to seeing what we haven't yet seen: our situation viewed through a fresh perspective. Not every date will lead to a committed relationship. But every date can inspire a deeper commitment to strengthening our skills in giving and receiving love. Not just in romantic relationships, but in relationships with everyone and everything we encounter.

Disclaimer and Terms of Use
This book is not intended for use as a source of medical advice.
All readers are advised to seek services of competent professionals
in the medical field as needed.

1.

Disintegration

When things fall apart...

Every life includes loss, and much of it is necessary. We lose the warmth of the womb in order to enter the world. We leave friends behind when we graduate from junior high to begin high school and again when we leave high school to attend university or to work. We leave our families of origin to begin families of our own. These changes are frequently bittersweet: We long to move forward but grieve what remains behind. Still, necessary losses are usually the result of our choices. But the loss of a primary relationship through an unexpected breakup, separation or divorce is a shock. Waves of deep sadness, relentless anger and terrifying anxiety crash endlessly into our days and nights. It's almost as if these difficult emotions now reside in the space our partner once occupied. We sleep restlessly, forget to eat, or we eat to stuff the pain. Sometimes it feels like we are dying. We fear that we will never love or be loved again. Of course, we will.

A breakup or divorce touches the raw edges of other unhealed wounds in our lives: fears of abandonment, of loneliness, even financial ruin. This is the experience of disintegration: the collapse of what we thought was true about ourselves as individuals and about our world. Perhaps we believed that our marriage was invincible or that we could never survive financially on our own or that our former partner was our soulmate. From a spiritual perspective, a relationship ends so that we can challenge the lies and limiting ideas we hold dear. By releasing these deceptions, we expand our consciousness and evolve into a more genuine version of ourselves. In the process, we discover new realities: We were in denial about our fragile marriage, we are completely capable of being financially responsible for ourselves, and the world is full of potential soulmates.

Dear Joey,

My heart is broken. I have been totally rejected by someone I love very much. I cannot eat or sleep. I cry all the time and feel punched in the stomach. How do I feel worthwhile again?

If you gave more of your time and life energy to the relationship than you gave to God or to your own life, you will feel like you are dying. But it is the relationship that has completed its life cycle and with it, one possible vision of yourself and your future. That means there is a new direction waiting for you. So grieve. Commit to counseling and to bodywork through this period of transformation. You will feel worthwhile again when you realize that this experience is what the spiritual teacher Don Bisson calls "a comma, not a period" on your life's journey.

Dear Joey,

I recently had a relationship break up with one of my best male friends. The last time we went out, he admitted he loved me. He kissed me passionately, and I just melted. That was three weeks ago, and since then, he never returns my calls. I'm angry, confused and sad. Even if nothing becomes of that kiss, I want him in my life. Did I do something wrong?

Well, you did something that seems unfair and that is to blame yourself for someone else's behavior. What if it's all about him and not all about you? Then you would miss an opportunity to be angry, confused and sad. Don't want to feel those emotions? Consider this: When sadness arises, how does your behavior change? For example, do you spend more time alone? Spend more time alone on a regular basis, and there will be less need to create difficult emotions and attach them to life experiences in order to justify your solitude. When we give ourselves what we need on a regular basis, we don't have to initiate dramatic emotions to force ourselves into self-care.

Notice, too, if you spun off after that delicious kiss into a happily-ever-after story. Forget fantasies. Meet reality by trusting that your friend is doing what is best for him. Then treat yourself with more gentleness and love.

Dear Joey,

My life partner died five years ago (we were together for 25 years). About a year ago, I met this wonderful guy (not perfect, but nice). I have emails that indicate our shared feelings. We even discussed living together. But after six months of dating, he threw me out of his life. I think he got scared when I said that I was falling in love with him. He refuses to discuss anything. I called his sister, and she said he uses people and that I deserved better. My head says good riddance, but my heart aches. I'm active in the community, but my heart is in pain. Part of it, I know, is that he refuses to talk. What can I do to forget this guy or force him to talk?

Emotional balance will return when you retrieve the focus you've placed on him and return it to you. Begin by dropping the idea that you can force him to talk. That effort carries a brutality that can inspire defensiveness and even dishonesty in the other person, because they believe they are under attack. The truth is, he's given you a response: silence. It's not your preference, but it's life's invitation to grow comfortable with not knowing why something happens while trusting that it's truly all good.

The generous gift of your heart was not received as expected. Is it possible that you did nothing wrong? Or that none of this is related to you telling him that you were falling in love? Take care not to use this experience to condition yourself to fear saying, "I love you," in the future. Heal yourself by stubbornly choosing to continue loving yourself and him as you both are, right now, in this situation. Doing so may not change the situation, but it will strengthen your heart. Remember, too, that you said he was "not perfect, but nice." Perhaps you were settling. If so, your heartache may be a signal to be patient. Let go of him, but do not abandon your hopes for the right partner.

Dear Joey,

I was in a relationship that was barely off the ground when it ended. My problem is that my pain is out of proportion to the trigger. I know this pain is about something much earlier in my life, but I can't pinpoint what it is or how to heal. This is not the first relationship that has enveloped me in abandonment. I've been involved in therapy, support groups and a wide variety of spiritual and emotional growth programs, but right now I feel that I have never learned anything from any of them. Where does this pain originate and how do I heal it?

The pain originates from inside you every time you abandon yourself in an effort to be loved by another. When you trim your real opinion or give away all of your personal time or daydream about a future together, you are rushing the relationship so that you can hurry up and get your needs met.

If you believe that love comes from others, you might be avoiding self-love. Sometimes we engage in manipulative little games and become so masterful at believing them that we actually think, when the games fail, something was done to us. Or we fear that something is deeply wrong with us. It's the rare person who is willing to plunge deeply into his or her own shadow and understand what they've done to themselves and the other. In my experience, it's further than most therapies, support groups or personal growth programs ever go.

So how do you heal? Let a relationship be one part of your life; don't remake your life around the relationship. Trust that neither the person nor the experience will vanish if you take care of yourself. Initiate a friendship with yourself. Discover the gift of abandonment: It forces you to return to you. So if you "stay home" (connected to your thoughts and feelings) while in relationship, you don't experience abandonment. Amazing, huh?

Dear Joey,

Is it possible for a guy who is emotionally unavailable to open up? My boyfriend is really smart, funny, likes my dog (important!) and is an amazing lover. But it seems like he picks a fight with me the day after every great date. I feel like I get so needy because he never meets me emotionally. He says that my neediness drives him away. He won't make a commitment to me, although he says he's not going anywhere. He is uncomfortable being physically affectionate in public, and I'm totally demonstrative. Is there any hope?

There is hope aplenty—right now—if you don't demand anything more than what you have or what he can freely give. But, yes, it is possible for someone who has been emotionally unavailable to open up—if he is willing. No amount of desire, encouragement, coddling or manipulation on your part will change anything. Willingness is the doorway because transforming a habit of self-protection requires a constant two-step of discipline and commitment. Of course, you can also practice being more emotionally available to yourself. If you are committed to meeting your own needs, you will, eventually, grow into a human being whose soul and ego are one.

Dear Joey,

My boyfriend has a woman friend who runs to him every time she breaks up with a guy. Since her rollercoaster relationships only last three months, she runs to him often. I told him that she uses him, but he says she's had a hard life. I don't like this woman, and I don't trust her. My boyfriend once had a thing for her, and I feel that she plays him. She knows that he and I are together, but she generally acts like I don't exist. She's quick to try to catch my boyfriend's eye, though, and loves to engage in inside jokes with him in my presence. Don't tell me to quit my boyfriend. I love him. Just help me deal.

He thinks she needs him. She thinks she needs him. Your choice is either to accept that or to minimize the importance of their relationship by emphasizing reality: You are the one he is dating. Enjoy that! Then have compassion for this woman. It's likely that her relationship with your boyfriend represents the only sustained relationship she has with a man. So she clings. Unfortunately, his Dr. Phil routine keeps her away from what she really needs: individual psychotherapy. In her book, Anatomy of the Spirit, Carolyn Myss writes about people who use their wounds to order and control relationships. "Without a schedule for healing, we risk becoming addicted to what we think of as support and compassion…it becomes extremely difficult to give up the privileges that accompany being wounded."

So don't fret. They don't have genuine emotional intimacy because no healing is taking place. They have wound intimacy. It provides an emotional charge through dependency, neediness and neurotic cycles of rescuing. Be concerned only if your boyfriend also runs to her with his troubles or if he shares emotional intimacies with her (about himself or you) that he does not share with you.

It's very third grade to engage in inside jokes in front of others. In her desperation to cling to him, she is trying to draw a boundary that leaves you out. Unfortunately, he is so stuck in their pattern that he fails to see that their behavior is inappropriate. You'll have to be the adult by smiling generously and asking your boyfriend for an explanation of the joke (if you ask her, she's likely to give him a coy look that will touch off another round of shared laughter). By doing so, you'll be including yourself. If they have a modicum of social grace between them, they will eventually include you or stop the secrets.

Dear Joey,

My boyfriend said that he is not ready to be in a serious relationship, so he broke up with me. We were together for over a year. He knows that he should be more committed and should say, "I love you," more often, but he is not ready for that level of commitment. He did say he loved me but not more than once a day because that was too much for him. He said there's a chance of getting back together when he figures out what he wants. What can I do to feel better (not cry all the time, or feel sick and depressed)? We're going on a trip we planned together with his family for a week. Should I try to remain platonic, or should I let things happen if it's going well?

A platonic relationship is one in which there is no romantic attraction or expectation. But you have a huge bundle of feelings for your ex, along with the hope of a renewed commitment. So platonic is not an option right now. The real question is whether you should go on vacation at all (Scary thought, huh?). If you must go, do the inner work necessary to release expectations. You must fully accept the relationship as it is (broken up) and possess no expectation of getting back together. While on vacation, check in with yourself at regular intervals. Don't engage in any action that is motivated by the belief that if you do this one thing, your boyfriend will return or even like you more. And even if you experience a strong connection with your ex, don't assume that it will lead anywhere. You can only gain if you are not afraid of losing.

Is it true that three little words would have saved your relationship? Saying "I love you" implies commitment and promise only if two people share the same definition of love, whether they are born to it or wrestle it out in a series of conversations. The reality is that genuine love is a decision, not a feeling. Most importantly, the words, "I love you," are not intended as pills to medicate our insecurities. "I love you" is not an incantation to reassure us that the relationship is still breathing or that we are still desirable. Those three little words actually fall short of expressing what a couple truly experiences as love.

Depression, tears, and anger are normal when a relationship dies. They signal the loss of dreams of the future created together during the relationship. So grieve. Then focus on what you have learned so you can live in the world, transformed and free.

Dear Joey,

My boyfriend of two years has cornered me into a dry, loveless relationship. In the beginning, I thought we had something valuable together, but he pulled away, eventually refusing sex (or any physical contact). He is now a friend who seeks me out for an occasional dinner date. When I express my desire for intimacy or ask if he would rather find a better mate, he cries and says he cares for me, but his former girlfriend's suicide broke something inside him, so I must accept the relationship on his terms. So he can't break up with me, and when I make the decision to leave him, a great sadness overcomes me. Am I deluding myself by trying to change him under the pretense of loving him? I feel he could provide the close relationship I ache for, but how patient should I be?

You've already been too patient! I want you to have the relationship you ache for. I want you to be loved and cherished by a man who has the capacity to give and receive love. But you have cornered yourself into believing that longing equals love, or the potential for it. That allows you to remain in denial. Now hear this: Everything this guy is doing shouts that he's not that into you. If he was, he would go to therapy and push himself beyond his past so he could be your guy. Clinging to him won't alter his refusal to change.

Here's another huge red flag: He is far too accomplished at playing wounded, and you are too skilled at being his accomplice. This man has not really been your boyfriend. The term "boyfriend" implies an emotional, spiritual, mental, and physical intimacy that your relationship with him lacks. You may feel attached to him, but attachment is not intimate. Attachment is often a sign of neediness, even addiction. By contrast, intimacy is the capacity to be open, honest and vulnerable with another human being.

The sadness that embraces you when you imagine a breakup is grief rising. It exists because you fear that the closure of your relationship with this man means the end of the dreams you had of a loving, committed union with anyone. Stop lying to yourself; this is not your only chance at love. You are also grieving the realization that your love does not magically change a man into someone who will love you back. Be glad for the eyes to see through that lie. It distracts you from admitting when a relationship is no longer working.

Dear Joey,

The girl I love left me. She says I'm angry and need counseling. I haven't acknowledged or dealt with the abuse in my past because it wasn't as bad as other people's abuse, but it makes me flighty and apt to get angry over small things. I was very mean to her. I look in the mirror, and I can't look at my own face because of some of the things that I did. I don't want her to be with someone else. I don't understand why she won't try again. I can't make her. I feel like she was my last chance. I don't understand why every time I find a great girl, I wreck it.

Oh, honey! How can you possibly expect to have a romantic relationship that is healthy when your history contains unmitigated abuse? It's like choosing to live with gangrene and then being shocked that amputation is necessary. Perhaps this time, your heartbreak is strong enough to catapult you into the realization that you need a qualified therapist to guide you out of the darkness.

The practice of comparing yourself to others and then issuing a decree ("They need therapy; their experience was much worse than mine.") allows you to continue living from your insecurity and need to feel better than others. Anyone who was abused as a child has experienced transgression by someone they should have been able to trust. The abused child becomes an adult who is tentative in relationships because he has learned that people are not safe enough to trust. Yet an enormous part of being fully human is establishing and maintaining healthy emotional intimacy. So you may find yourself driven toward intimacy with a woman and then pulling back awkwardly and unexpectedly because of your history of abuse. At times, you will use drama—like getting angry over minor things—as an excuse to exit the date, day or relationship. The majority of this anger is emotion that was not expressed when the abuse occurred (How could it be? You were a child.). The remaining anger arises to hide the fear of immersion in intimacy. A part of you believes, incorrectly, that you must protect yourself because you have been so hurt. That belief is an obstacle. Genuine love is born when we are open and vulnerable. The good news is there is always another chance. However, it may not be with the person we expect.

One way to begin loving, now, is to go to therapy. Another is to support your former girlfriend in her choice not to continue the relationship. As a man who has been abused, you certainly can understand why someone would want to exit an abusive relationship. If you truly love her, you want the best for her, even if that means she decides (in the future) to be with someone else.

Dear Joey,

My girlfriend broke up with me, but I'm still in love with her. I try not to fight the sadness and pain—if I feel like crying, I let myself cry—but an ache remains. I feel too incomplete by myself to be with anyone else. I could use any thoughts or suggestions you have.

Surrendering to your tears is a compassionate gesture; saltwater is very healing. Some people consider tears to be a sign of suffering. But I know them, too, as a way that the Divine moves in us. Tears soften our ego armature and prepare us for spiritual, mental, emotional and physical rebirth.

Let's tend to what inspires your tears. This wound, the ache that now holds your attention, could it also be perceived as an opening? Perhaps the you that existed in the relationship refused the width of your true self. Sometimes, through interactions with others, we glimpse our own holiness even as we struggle first to believe what we see and then to contain it before anyone else sees it (We can't possibly be that big or luminous, we mutter to ourselves!). The fear is that if we're seen as luminous, we may be challenged to live from that enlightened space.

Intimate relationships reveal the extent to which we have given of ourselves to ourselves. Only after you possess yourself can you truly love another without feeling incomplete in their absence. How then to be your own beloved? As the High Priestess who served as the Oracle at Delphi said to Socrates, "Know thyself." Yes, own your blessedness. As you integrate, remember: The experience of perceived separation from that which you love may feel like the impact of the Big Bang. But every Big Bang is followed by the creation of new life. Trust that transformation to a wider, truer you is underway.

Dear Joey,

My girlfriend and I argue a lot. One of the big problems is my insecurity. I try to overcome it, but the more we argue, the more insecure I get. I pray for an answer but get none. I don't want to continue our destructive cycle of arguing, but I am also scared to leave her.

Insecurity is the fruit of believing that what other people think, say, do or who they appear to be is more delicious than anything you could ever be, have or do. If allowed to ripen, these beliefs loom into fears that others are superior and will take what little love you have. Arguing, then, is a natural outgrowth of insecurity because you think that you must, at any cost, hang on to what you believe is yours. But if you pay attention to your own life, you can nourish who you really are and create the life you long to inhabit. First, though, get to the core belief where your insecurity roots. It's a slippery task. Here's why: Insecurity means that you've been lying to yourself for a long time. So it's helpful to have professional support to locate the original lie that is continually reseeding itself in your thoughts. A gifted psychotherapist or spiritual director can guide you.

Dear Joey,

For nearly three years, I dated a much younger man. We got along great, had fantastic sex, and considered ourselves a couple. Several months ago he left saying he loved me but not our age difference. I'm dating now but having trouble letting go emotionally. I've prayed, done Tarot and closure ceremonies but still feel an ache where my heart was.

Stop treating your heart like a phantom limb. Pretending that it is excised hurts your spirit, and right now you need the insights that your sweet spirit can provide. After all, that ache may be your heart's way of saying, "I'm still here, alive—can you feel me?" Sometimes when experiences do not match expectations, we want to believe that we are irreparably damaged. It's a romantic notion that is not reality-based. So don't focus on the pain, focus on what it calls you to—a chance to re-examine and realign yourself with your life purpose.

Dear Joey,

My fiancé and I broke up after he slept with one of my friends. I am still reeling, even though he didn't treat me very well before he cheated. He talked down to me, and I never felt good, but we were living together and it just seemed like it would work out. My family keeps asking when I'm going to get married (I'm 32). I don't know what to say. I've dealt with all of this by staying drunk for a year. I'm so afraid I will always be alone.

Oh, sweetie! You've already discovered that staying drunk prolongs pain; it doesn't help you hurdle it. As long as you deny painful feelings, you are at their mercy. Buried feelings don't dissipate; they emerge at inopportune times to level you, to bleed out awkwardly in ordinary interactions with people, and to encourage you toward behaviors that create a chaotic life. Healing begins when you stop drinking. You must be sober to successfully exit this betrayal. After a year of staying drunk, you need Alcoholics Anonymous to be clear-headed enough to work through your past. Don't be afraid to reach out.

Although it might sound blasphemous now, you will be grateful someday that your fiancé and friend betrayed you. After all, you were about to marry a man you knew you should not marry. His disrespect was a ginormous red flag, but in the face of family pressure to marry and your fears of being alone, you clung to a relationship that kept you stunted emotionally. That's the main reason the betrayal hurts: You betrayed yourself (who you are, the depth of love that you are capable of giving and receiving) in order to remain engaged.

The next time that your family inquires about a wedding date, don't get defensive. Just smile. You're not doing anything wrong by waiting to get to know yourself well enough to choose a suitable partner. This is the 21st century; marriage is not the only lifestyle choice. If you fear being alone, begin to embrace the experience of time spent in solitude. After you shift past the fears of being lonely, you will discover the joy of time spent enjoying your own company. Then you will understand a universal reality: If we are all connected, you are never alone.

Dear Joey,

My boyfriend and I did the long distance thing for a year. We knew it was too hard and broke up two months ago. He initiated the breakup, and a part of me is trying to deal with feelings of rejection. I am an attractive person, with a strong career and financial independence, and a good number of friends. I am trying to keep busy, even trying to date, but I still feel so sad sometimes. Is this normal? I'll do fine for a week or so, then suddenly I'll just miss him terribly and feel so sad. Sometimes I'll go home and just cry for hours until I fall asleep. I thought it would be good for me to buy myself an adult toy. But when I use it, it just makes me cry and miss him even more. Is there something exceptionally wrong with me?

Actually, there is something profoundly right in your willingness to experience your feelings. Emotions offer information and a direction. Your body is focusing your attention toward what needs healing. The work is to trace those feelings back to the beliefs that inspired them. For example, perhaps before you go home and cry yourself to sleep, you think "(his name here) always called me when I got off work." Since you know he is not going to call, you sink into a deepening sadness. Other thoughts feed it: "Men always leave me. I'll never have what I want." Soon you're soaking your pillow again.

It is difficult to strip our psyche of its veils. But seeing the truth about ourselves heals and strengthens us. That brings me to your inclination to play with toys. Remember, the toy doesn't have the power to make you cry and miss your ex-boyfriend. It's more likely that when you masturbate, you are reminded that what you really crave is intimacy. A toy can't provide that. And, the truth is, what you actually need right now is to be emotionally and spiritually intimate with yourself. So whenever you label your feelings as loss, take time to elicit the fears beneath your sadness. Then, put fear to rest through talk therapy, journaling or meditation. It's also helpful to discontinue dating until this healing process is complete. That's being kind to yourself and to the men you meet.

Dear Joey,

I got back together with an old boyfriend, even though I knew better. At the time, I was raw from other problems and in no mood to play mind games. I said that if he wasn't sincere about giving me the kind of relationship I needed, he should move on. He knew that I didn't really trust him and begged me to. He insisted that he wanted only me. In our previous relationship, I knew I loved him but learned to live with him not really wanting me. This time he courted me. I believed him when he said that he loved me. Now he says he's married to his job. I deserve better. I am shell-shocked because there was an element of deceit involved. I'm so embarrassed and hurt that I can barely function. I don't dare tell my parents. Please help.

It's tantalizing to read, "…there was an element of deceit involved." Did you deceive yourself by hooking up "even though you knew better"? Or by knowing that you were "in no mood to play mind games" yet entering a relationship where thriving with your brain in knots was a requirement? Or by being emotionally intimate with a man you didn't trust? Or by failing to ask yourself whether you were sincere about giving yourself the kind of relationship that you needed? Or realizing that your relationship with your parents doesn't allow you to tell them the truth?

I understand that you believed it when he said that he loved you. But I bet that you had to talk yourself into it, and in that process, you repeatedly tucked away the small signs and questions that insisted it really wasn't different this time around.

You've been at war with yourself for so long that feeling shell-shocked is natural. Stop handing this man ammunition to use against you. Heal the neediness that accepts affection from others at any cost to you. Your ex is right about one thing: You deserve better.

Dear Joey,

My soulmate was recently divorced when we met and unexpectedly fell in love. He wasn't ready for a commitment. He was seeing other women. That really hurt me, so we mutually decided to put space between us while he healed. I feel so empty. Even a simple conversation with friends becomes tedious and my mind wanders. I'm seeing a counselor but want your opinion. Is it possible to reconnect with a lost soulmate?

You already are. Through the pain of this experience you seek a deeper understanding of yourself. This is one step toward discovering that you are your own true soulmate. Once you accept that responsibility, connecting deeply with another becomes the norm, rather than the exception. Your heart widens through every encounter with the world and what moves in it. That inspires you to not expect anyone other than yourself to carry the burden of your needs, wants, desires and happiness. If someone arrives in your life, as this friend did, and there's a connection, you can enjoy it. If the relationship ends, your sense of balance doesn't.

Expanding into wholeness...

When everything falls apart, it's an invitation to accept a powerful reality: Everything happens for our spiritual evolution. To heal from a breakup, separation or divorce requires that we grieve and then open our mind and heart to embrace the death of the relationship. This is easier to do after we have passed out of the habit of resisting our new life in the present. In the process, we learn that asking "why" does not transform suffering. Transformation begins when we explore our suffering with curiosity and compassion, seeking the lessons of love and wisdom hidden inside the pain.

2.

Cheating

Only cheaters think love is a game...

Infidelity is a searing wound to the heart. The shock of betrayal pitches the mind backward, scouring each day, searching for missed clues about the affair's beginning or end. A litany of self-blame loops though our thoughts as we swing between excruciating sadness and extraordinary fury at our partner's selfishness. Often it doesn't matter whether our partner was involved in a one-night stand or an ongoing relationship or an emotional affair. The truth is infidelity forces us to question everything we believed in, even ourselves.

Against these odds, we must still commit to being our own advocates. Life, at its core, is choice-making about giving and receiving love. Cleave to this reality. It serves as a guide to allow the experience of unfaithfulness to ultimately inspire a new self and an expansive existence. We can then move forward with a heart enlarged by our own capacity to continue loving ourselves through trauma and out the other side. That's when we can celebrate the triumph of knowing what we will no longer tolerate in relationships. And we experience the joy of trusting that we will meet a more perfect match.

This journey is much easier if we avoid engaging in behaviors often hyped as normal in movies, songs and other collective fantasies. To learn to love honestly:

Don't Play Sherlock Holmes: Forget the amateur detective routine. Don't search for more clues about this or other affairs. Don't interrogate your partner. Obsessively asking questions makes you appear desperate, insecure, even paranoid. If you know your partner cheated, your relationship is in trouble. Details don't make a difference.

Don't Blame Your Partner's Fling: Focusing your anger at the person your partner cheated with is unproductive. It feeds your denial about the ill health of your relationship. Think of it this way: Who made the commitment to be faithful to you? That's the person who violated your trust and betrayed your heart.

Don't Blame Yourself: Your partner didn't cheat because you are not enough. Your partner cheated because he or she cheats. It has little or nothing to do with you and everything to do with your partner's failings.

Vow now to affair-proof your next relationship by choosing a partner who values honesty, trustworthiness and fidelity as much as you do. Care more about yourself than the person who cheated on you by accepting an apology, if it is offered, but not returning to the relationship unless you fully accept the possibility of future betrayals. Yes, a startling number of affairs thread through the lives of couples today. But you don't have to be among them unless you want to be.

Dear Joey,

My boyfriend has repeatedly lied to me. He said that he was 23 and only had one child. Later, I found out that he was 28 with two children. Then a girl confessed that she had been messing around with him for months. He denied it, but in my heart I knew that it was true. I got over that, and we moved on. Months later, he didn't want to have sex. Finally, he confessed that he had cheated on me with a few girls, and he was currently cheating on me with someone. I really didn't know how to handle the hurt. So I slept with an ex-boyfriend one time. I confessed and said I did it because he wasn't being intimate with me. We got over that and moved on. Recently, I was at his house and read a text message from a girl. I called her back, and she told me that they had been dating for over a year. I don't think he really loves me. We are constantly arguing, breaking up and getting back together. I love him, but I'm tired of his games. He told me today that he doesn't want to be with me right now. I want to move on with my life and meet someone nice, but I really do love him. What should I do?

Love yourself enough to leave. Not everyone we love or think we love is a good partner for us. And, of course, it's likely you're not in love at all. Sometimes those big feelings are what we already have inside of us. We project that love onto another person and imagine the feelings are because of him or her. Other times what we call love is actually infatuation or pseudo-love. Infatuation is an intense rush of attraction that convinces us we are in love even when the relationship lacks trust, commitment, or even the basic qualities of friendship. We can also be driven by childhood wounds to recreate unhealthy relationship patterns. These painful, rollercoaster relationships can be transformed if both people are devoted to self-reflection and change. But when there are continuous lies and betrayals and commitment is never a priority, it's time to say goodbye.

Before dating anyone new, study the art of relationship. Focus on understanding true intimacy. People who are uncomfortable with the word "sex" use the word intimacy as a euphemism for sexual activity. Let's be clear: Engaging in sex does not magically create emotion, connection or love. Intimacy is built slowly, over time, through honest communication, trust, care and compassion. So in the future, be certain to develop the essentials of true friendship—spiritual, mental and emotional intimacy— before giving yourself to someone sexually. Doing so will help you to keep your mind clear enough to choose more wisely.

Dear Joey,

I think my girlfriend is cheating on me with another woman. She was involved with a woman before me, and I checked her phone and found texts that it's happening again. It's all I think about. I don't want to lose her.

Why not, honey? If your suspicions prove true, let go of her. She released you long ago to make room for her new squeeze. And don't you want to be with someone who loves you and lives it? Give her a wide berth and sail on with your bad self. With so much real love available in the world, there's no need to tolerate the counterfeit stuff.

Dear Joey,

It's 3:21 a.m., and I can't sleep because I realize that I am head over heels for a co-worker. The problem is that I have a girlfriend I love very much. I pride myself on only using the word "love" when I really mean it. Our relationship has been very smooth, and I trust her more than anyone. She is a blessing to me because I had given up on finding someone honest. So now I am the biggest hypocrite in the world because I am thinking about letting go of her to pursue this other woman. I am afraid to spend time alone with my co-worker because when I do, I am sick to my stomach. She doesn't know it, but she opens up feelings for me that my girlfriend can't. I am ashamed of how I feel and wish we'd never met. I have never let someone go (it's always been the other way around), and I am afraid to hurt my girlfriend. I know it's not lust. Is this a test of my faith?

You write that your girlfriend is a blessing. That word actually means "to wound." Certainly those who are nearest and dearest have an awesome ability to wound our egos. For the insightful among us, that kind of wound can inspire the blessing of learning how to love and be loved. But if we are not ready for such a delicious shift, we elevate our partners to superior positions over us (perhaps believing that they can see us more clearly than we see ourselves) and ruin our potential for equality in relationship. Or, when the relationship is so intimate that wounding is possible, we run away—first, emotionally and then, physically. If your relationship with your girlfriend is as sweet as you say, it may also be scary because it holds a promise of increased intimacy, intensified commitment, contentment and no drama. For some people (you, perhaps?), an easy, joyful relationship creates a stack of worries between the ears. Hey, instead of pursuing your coworker, consider challenging yourself to surrender into what you have. Train your brain to stop obsessing about the woman you work with by bringing every thought back into the present moment whenever your mind drifts into a daydream. Eventually, you will know whether you are running away from the blessings in your life or if you are ready for someone new.

Dear Joey,

Why are men such dogs? I found my boyfriend up in my house with another woman, half-naked. When I confronted them, he told her that I was his roommate! I threw his clothes and hers out the door and told them to go. He lost his job last June, and I have been supporting us. He said that he wanted to take classes so that he could get a better job and we could get married. I told all my friends that I was getting married. I am so embarrassed to let anyone know what happened. My boyfriend has been calling me and leaving messages about how much he misses me. He says that she didn't mean anything to him and he only loves me. My heart is broken, and I need your advice. I miss him. What should I do?

You should remember that if men are dogs, it's because we (you, me, the culture, parents, neighbors, teachers, clergy) have taught them to disrespect women. Don't contribute to that bad education by bringing your ex-boyfriend back into your life. If he did love you, he would have made himself worthy by getting a job and courting you properly. He would have proven that he is reliable, truthful and trustworthy. But in the moment that you caught him cheating, he called you his roommate. He was more concerned about protecting his relationship with the other woman than about reassuring you. His current circumstances (jobless, without a home) are motivating his phone seduction. You deserve better. Change your locks and phone number, grieve the betrayal, and move on.

Dear Joey,

I have great chemistry with my boyfriend of two years; we enjoy each other's company a lot. My problem is that he lives with his ex-girlfriend. They have lived together for 16 years and claim that they have had no relationship for the past four years (except as roommates). I asked my boyfriend to invite her to move and just be friends. They are very close friends and are very familiar with each other. She is always in his bedroom using his computer. She shops, cooks, cleans, does his laundry and mows the lawn in exchange for a lowered rent. He said he has asked her to move, and she is taking her time. She lives off a small trust fund and doesn't work. He is retired. I work full time. He is from a culture that has a history of men having more than one wife. I had decided to set a boundary to move on after two years, but I am having trouble following through. He wants his roommate to move out at her own pace, but it just doesn't seem to happen. I feel like a fool for staying with him. Am I controlling and rigid, or is this is a legitimate beef?

Is it controlling and rigid to request that your boyfriend change his living arrangements? No. Is it rigid and controlling to hide your legitimate concerns beneath the issue of your boyfriend's roommate? Yes. You are being unkind to yourself by denying your true fears. The real question is: Where is this relationship going? It sounds like you want a deeper commitment, the certainty of exclusivity, and a promise of a future with your boyfriend. You believe that if this woman were out of sight, she would be out of mind, too. Let me suggest that if your boyfriend had the intention of being genuinely committed to you, he would take your request and deadline seriously. Of course, if you were genuinely committed to you, you would take your request and deadline seriously, too.

If your boyfriend respected your deadline, he would lose a woman comfortable in her roles as his wife and mother. If you respect your deadline, you risk losing him. You want him to make a choice, but your fear says: If you let him go, you may not find anyone else with whom you have such great chemistry. Stop investing in scarcity thinking. Have the courage to challenge your fears, and move on to create what you truly desire.

Dear Joey,

I fell in love with a co-worker, quite by accident. We seemed to always be on break together sharing lively, witty and profound conversations that we now enjoy over lunch or dinner. The problem is that he is married. I am in my late 40s, never married and religious. But I would give up anything to be with him. He has shared details of his marriage and family life (three kids), and I have provided advice. Still, I hope that he will see that we really belong together. We have a chaste friendship, but I want more. Should I tell him that I love him?

If your love for him is narrow, you will tell him that you love him. But if your love for him is wide, you will seek only to support him in his commitment to his marriage, his family, his God and himself. Narrow love is self-serving and provides a foundation for drama and suffering. By contrast, love that is wide enough to be unconditional (you love him whether or not he returns that love) engenders liberation and grace for all who give or receive it.

So if you find yourself imagining a romantic future with your friend, stop. Be present with the relationship as it is. This will eventually inspire satisfaction and peace within you. You might also consider this: If you have not had relationships with men that are physically platonic but mentally and emotionally intimate, then engaging in conversational intimacy with a man may be confusing to you. It needn't be. Consider this relationship your invitation to understand that men and woman can be just friends, with no romantic or sexual energy attached.

Dear Joey,

I have been seeing a married man for several years and recently learned that he is also seeing someone else. I knew his tendency so it doesn't bother me. I want to continue our relationship. Am I crazy, or is this type of situation becoming more common and acceptable in society? I would like a family of my own but have not found anyone who is as compatible with me as he is. I don't want him to change. I just want him to love me. What do you think? Please answer in writing so I can show it to him.

I think that you want more than love from this man—you want marriage and a family. If that's true, be honest about it. Otherwise, you're just tucking in parts of yourself, trying to be emotionally neat and presentable, to appeal to him. Eventually, your buried desires will unravel and have a tantrum, probably at an inopportune time. If this man is still married to his current wife when you realize that you want more, you'll want to tell him—and her. That's a ticket to a drama of operatic proportions.

It's easy to be detached about his extramarital affairs when you are not his spouse. Right now, your desire for him is so big that it may obscure your ability to be honest. As for sharing a man, oh, it's been accepted in many cultures throughout recorded history. But in the 21st century, the only way to determine acceptability is to engage in transparency. That means everyone, including his wife, knows who is having sex with whom. This is healthy for the body as well as the mind. The heart, however, usually prefers a more traditional one-to-one commitment.

One last thing, your interest in your friend seeing this question published doesn't feel clean. It's as if you're trying to prove to him that you like him best and that it's you who accepts him, as is. If that isn't already clear in the relationship, seeing it in print is useless.

Dear Joey,

I have a boyfriend who has slept with other women a number of times since we have been together. I am still with him because I believe in love and forgiveness and have seen a lot of positive growth in his life. But I feel I am compromising myself because I want a monogamous relationship, and he cannot commit to that right now. I sometimes wonder if monogamy is something our society created from religious foundations for purposes of ownership. What should I do?

There is a line in the Tao Te Ching that reads: "When there is no desire, all things are at peace." The man in your life lives according to his impulsive desires. He is incapable of a monogamous relationship. Driven by lust, he is not able to love you. You have attached yourself to him. Your feelings for him are not love. If you loved yourself, you could admit this.

I want you to be more generous with yourself. Pour your heart into giving yourself the opportunity for monogamy. It doesn't matter what society or religion says about your choice. Here's what is important: You feel a call to a fully committed connection with a man. Stop forgiving him for disrespecting his relationship with you. Forgive him for being himself, and be grateful that you can now see the truth and move on.

Dear Joey,

I had an affair with a woman who practices at the same yoga studio that I do. She's married, I'm divorced (five years) and although I liked the sex, I never wanted a relationship with her. She's a lot older than me and not really my type. I was clear about this when she pushed for contact beyond just getting together for sex. When I said no, she stormed off. The next thing I know she calls me three weeks later and says that she told her husband about the affair and he wants to talk to me. I refused but ran into him outside the studio one day. He said that he wanted to thank me because the affair and me dumping his wife was the best thing ever for their marriage. They're like newlyweds again, he said. The problem is that I feel really weird about the whole thing now and can't get her out of my mind.

That's because she's got the muscle now. When you were in the position of being desired by her but only responding when you wanted your itch scratched, you felt powerful. Sadly, your ego translated that experience as positive. But lording power over someone else is unhealthy and unkind. So is disrespecting the boundaries of a committed relationship. If you were a man of integrity, your willingness to question her proposition might have been the prompt she needed to talk to her husband. Yes, it is possible that their marital issues could have been resolved without all the intermittent drama and corresponding adrenaline rushes. Are you willing to live in a world with that much peace?

The good news is that, at some level, you chose the affair so you could see a truth about yourself. Fear of intimacy leads people to have affairs. A person in a committed relationship may believe that it's much easier to seek satisfaction outside of a marriage than to observe, admit and alter how she or he contributes to the relationship's problems. And you might believe it is easier to control intimacy by only engaging in sex, rather than being vulnerable to the wholeness of the mind, spirit, body connection that true relationship demands from us. But I believe you're ready to be a true lover—a person who cares selflessly for others. The question is do you believe in your capacity to love?

Dear Joey,

The woman I love had an affair. I wanted to be done, but she convinced me that she made a mistake, so I agreed to forgive her. She made it clear to the other man that she wants me. I'm in my 50s and have never felt so in love. The problem is that she still has the other man in her life. He calls to cry on her shoulder. I feel foolish that I am here but love her enough to work through this. Is it unreasonable to want her to stop talking with him?

It is unreasonable to deny the truth: She has not given him up. Affairs are spurred by neediness or lust or an inability to sustain intimacy in the primary relationship or the dearth of courage to end a relationship that is not working (betrayal forces closure). When an affair ends, there should be no contact, perhaps ever, but at least for one year to allow the primary relationship to heal. People prone to affairs are often addicted to the adrenaline hits that cheating offers. Your girlfriend's willingness to remain the confidante of her ex-lover is a continuation of the betrayal, only now it's emotional.

Dear Joey,

My 40-year-old boyfriend slept with a 24-year-old, party girl co-worker shortly after he and I talked about purchasing a home together. We have kids from previous relationships, and I wanted us to be together as a family. After a six-week separation, he returned. I foolishly agreed to be his secret lover knowing he was dating this girl. Our energy was intense. We connected spiritually in a way that we never had before. I figured that he needed time to get what drove him to her out of his system. He apologized, said I was the right choice, and he wanted me in his life forever. A week later, he said he is having a baby with this girl but wants to be friends with me. I feel that he will regret this terrible mistake. I'm devastated and trying hard to stay positive. Meditation helps, but how do I deal with being without the love of my life?

By admitting that if you were the love of his life, he would not treat you with such utter disrespect. The joint purchase of a house is an invitation to a deeper commitment. Faced with that possibility, a rational adult would respond to his or her partner directly by saying: "Yes", "No" or "Maybe. I need to think about it for a week (or whatever period of time feels right)." For some people, buying a house with their partner is a life-changing opportunity, one that forces them to face the truth about their relationship. Your boyfriend clearly struggled with ambivalence about his relationship with you. But rather than acknowledge his concerns rationally and respectfully, he opted out by acting out. So don't employ a euphemism to soften the vagary of his affair: He didn't sleep with a co-worker. They had sex, and it was a betrayal of his commitment to you. Do you think he is the right man to teach your children about love?

Here is the truth: Your boyfriend dated his co-worker to get you out of his system. Once he felt free, he allowed himself to connect with you sexually. Since you yearned for a sign that he would choose you and not her, you imagined that sexual intercourse equaled emotional union. You had makeup sex with him while he was having breakup sex with you. The connection was intense because the union between you was dying. It felt spiritual because you imbued it with hope. Now it's time to be grateful that this relationship has ended. Mourn the closure and then become the love of your own life so you can understand what love should really feel like.

Dear Joey,

I told my girlfriend from the start that I was married but separated. She insisted that I get a divorce. I told her that I would try. We had a good relationship. I thought that I would marry her after my divorce. I did not count on legitimate delays, like my ex-wife getting pregnant by her new man. I felt an ethical obligation to my ex-wife, even though the baby was not mine. If I divorced her, her medical costs during the pregnancy would not be insured. Tired of excuses, my girlfriend dumped me. I felt that the only thing I could do was lie and say that I had filed for divorce. In an attempt to be open, I told her about my ex-wife's pregnancy. My girlfriend figured out that I lied. She accused me of lying about my divorce and cheating on her with my ex-wife and on my ex-wife with her. She also accused me of fathering my ex's baby. She has sent me nasty emails. I want to get back with her, but her trust in me has vanished. Is there any hope?

There is always hope. For example, I hope that you realize that lying destroys trust. I hope that you understand that you do not deserve a second chance with your girlfriend because you are not ready for a committed partnership. Separation is either a period of discernment (you are deciding whether to divorce or to work to mend the marriage) or a period of preparation (you're certain that divorce is the right choice, and you are moving toward it with clear, consistent actions and waiting before getting involved with someone else). If you are in discernment, you should not be dating; you should be in therapy. If you are dating, you and your nearly ex-spouse should be divvying knickknacks and meeting with an attorney to hash out the divorce. A person who is separated, but dating without moving toward divorce, is emotionally impotent. In your situation, keeping your ex-wife insured may have been an act of kindness. However, you may have done it to assuage your guilt about divorcing or about having an affair. Or your ego may have liked the feeling of her relying on you. The bottom line is that if you were planning to marry your girlfriend, you should have been acting like a couple. Yes, that means you would have told her everything. Then, as partners, you would have decided whether to keep your wife insured. You didn't. Your girlfriend's exit is the result of your betrayals.

Dear Joey,

I just broke up with my fiancée after finding out that she was running around with one of my friends. I lost her and him, too, and can't believe that they would do this to me. It also seems like other people knew about it and deliberately chose not to tell me. I feel like leaving and not telling anyone and never coming back. I really need your help.

Your impulse to run is not just emotional. Trauma activates the fight-or-flight area of the brain. And, after being abandoned by your fiancée and friend, your heart yearns to abandon them and the city where the pain began. But leaving does not guarantee that your suffering will disappear. You will carry that wounded heart with you wherever you land on this beautiful planet. So instead of running, let yourself feel the mountain of emotions attached to this situation. Grieve the betrayal and loss. Yes, that means expressing yourself in productive ways like crying or writing in a journal. You must also process your feelings by talking to a trusted friend or a talented psychotherapist. Don't contact your former fiancée or your former friend, though. Focus your energy on transforming into the next evolution of the man you know yourself to be. Let this trauma be the launch pad for a triumph of startling proportions.

Dear Joey,

My girlfriend monitors everything I do. From the beginning, she snooped around my Facebook page and questioned me. She justifies her irrational thinking with stereotypes, like: "All men have something to hide." Instead of focusing on things like obtaining gainful employment, she focuses on "the relationship" and accuses me of cheating. I tell her that I cannot be with some clingy, insecure, emotionally dependent little girl who constantly needs reassurance. Yet, she continues her childish behavior. I never pressure her for sex. She always wants sex and says I should always be ready. If I'm not, she thinks I've been having sex with someone else. I tell her that I would be attracted to her if she would cease the accusations. Should I just subjugate my emotions and perform for her benefit? Is it worth giving in if it makes me miserable?

You write that you have never pressured your girlfriend for sex. Why then, are you harassing yourself about it? Your obsessive pattern of thinking is twin to your girlfriend's pattern. So you argue with yourself in your mind, and you argue with your girlfriend when you are out of your mind. Oh, not literally, of course! But a person must be out of his conscious mind to argue so often about the same issues.

Problems arise in any relationship, but in a healthy relationship, difficulties are processed and solved. In those partnerships, each individual shares his or her feelings and perspective as the other listens. Then they switch roles. Next, the couple talks through the dilemma together and finds a viable solution. Sometimes that solution includes making changes to accommodate their partners. That's what real love does: invites us to become our best self.

Your situation is challenging because the basic elements necessary for a healthy relationship are missing: chemistry, friendship, trust and commitment. Relationships like yours are often the result of getting sexually involved too early, before you really know each other. For some people, sex is like glue. Even if the sex is not spectacular, they stay or at least remain peripherally connected. That's because sex stimulates the body's attachment chemicals. So even though the relationship is not working, our biology compels us to go back for more. Even when an evolved brain says, "Leave!" the body insists, "Stay!" Those mixed signals result in conflicted actions like constantly breaking up and getting back together, or in arguments that become fights, and fights that involve law enforcement.

You must have a serious conversation with the man in the mirror (yes, honey, that would be you). Start here: If your girlfriend never trusted you, why did you continue dating? This question is not an opportunity to judge yourself harshly. It's a way to explore your motivations. Only through honest inquiry can you awaken to how you have created a lifestyle that is painful to live. And if you and your girlfriend have children together, you must go to counseling. If you don't parent together, move on. She deserves someone she can trust. And so do you.

Dear Joey,

My girlfriend (we've lived together for ten years) is really close to this guy she works with. When I confronted her about cheating, she said they are just friends and that he is her "work husband." I've asked her for years to marry me, but she won't. Do you think she is involved with this guy?

Yes and no. Obviously, she has an emotional connection with this man, but that doesn't mean their relationship is a threat. A work spouse is a co-worker who is invested in your career but who is not a part of your life outside the office. Work spouses are committed to helping each other advance in their chosen professions. The pair tends to be within a few years of each other in age and at similar places in their careers. The relationship is closest to peer mentoring; each person alternates the coaching role in order to guide the other safely through office politics.

If the idea of a work spouse bothers you, investigate why. Do you question whether adults can have friendships outside of their primary relationship? Here's the reality: It's rare, but possible. Platonic friendships do exist between adults who might be partners if one or both was not already committed. But, honestly, what many people called a platonic friendship is a cover for an attraction-in-embryo. Another question: Do you trust your partner to be mature enough to respect appropriate boundaries regarding emotional intimacy? It's true: Work spouse relationships can be gateways into affairs. However, that doesn't happen if the work spouses maintain the devotion to their romantic partners. After all, anyone who is intent on having an affair will do so. An affair is not about opportunity. Most affairs result from an attachment to dishonesty. People who are dissatisfied with themselves and their current relationships but lack the backbone to admit it and change are at risk for an affair. Does that situation fit your girlfriend?

Your girlfriend's unwillingness to wed does mean that she struggles with trust and commitment. That is a greater threat to your future and long-term happiness together than a work spouse. If marriage is the lifestyle choice you desire, accept that she is not the woman for you. As painful as it may become, either ditch your dream of marriage or dump your girlfriend. Find a woman capable of saying "yes" when invited to share your life.

Dear Joey,

My 15-year-old son told me that my wife is having an affair. I told him that I trust my wife and don't believe it. I didn't even let him finish. I have not spoken to my wife about this. My son gets along well with me but is sullen and disrespectful toward his mom. My wife keeps talking about the difficulty of having a teenager in the house. My son says my wife is sexting some guy she works with, and he read the messages (now erased). My son tells me daily that he hates his mom. The tension between them is unbearable. I am not sure what to do.

Listen to your son so he feels understood. His hostility toward your wife will continue until he is guided into releasing his feelings in a constructive way. Instead of denying the possibility of your wife's affair, listen to your son's fears that his mother is having an affair. Can you grasp the difference? Your son is scared that his mother is not who she says she is, that his family structure might be radically altered, and that his father is asleep at the wheel. When he mustered the courage to talk about these fears, your response was to push him away. In terms of your relationship with your son, it doesn't matter whether you are cuckolded. What is important is that his feelings are heard, that his worries are received without overreaction from you, and that he is reassured that sharing his fears with a caring adult is a good choice.

It's possible that your son is right. It's also conceivable that he liked or dated someone who cheated on him, and he is projecting that pain. Projection is a defense mechanism. We unconsciously engage in projection when we deny feelings, thoughts or traits of our own and imagine other people are lugging that baggage.

Your rejection of your son's fear reveals some denial in you. An unwillingness to listen may mean you carry a shred of suspicion, too. That feeling isn't evidence that your wife is cheating, of course. But it is a nudge signifying that you have a little housecleaning to do (in your mind and heart, that is).

Dear Joey,

My wife found an old boyfriend on Facebook. She told me when it happened. I didn't mind because I trusted her. Now she says they are in love. She wants a divorce. I am convinced that she is having a fantasy. I told her that I would separate, temporarily, so she could see this guy (he lives in another state) and get this out of her system. The next day she moved out. Did I do the wrong thing?

Your wife believes the stars have aligned to reunite her with her soulmate. You called it a fantasy. To her mind that means you don't get it. In other words, you minimized her feelings, so she assumes you are in denial or jealous of her true love. Where does all of this leave you? Taking good care of yourself, I hope. Don't hold on to someone who wants to leave you. But do try this: Focus all of your attention on listening to her. When she is talking about this other man, their relationship or plans, put your own fears and concerns aside and just listen. Be happy that she is happy. Tell her that you love her and all you want is for her to be happy. Be the guy she forgot you are. Long-distance relationships wane when you find yourself living in the same town with the man you really love (yes, darlin', that would be you).

Dear Joey,

A handsome but married consultant attended a work-related meeting at my home. He and I had chatted previously and discovered amazing connections. After the meeting he lingered. I cleaned up after he left and discovered a cell phone. Early the next morning, he called about the phone. Two minutes later the doorbell rang. I was still in my bathrobe. I handed him the phone, but he pulled the door open and stepped in. He didn't want to leave. I'm attracted but don't want to cross the line. His wife is pregnant with twins. Do you think he is trying to start an affair?

It's possible that he's just a friendly, forgetful person. Or he could be a guy with no sense of appropriate boundaries. But he is probably a man who is aching because he is no longer the center of his wife's attention. Many people are startled to discover the selflessness that parenting demands. The transition can be particularly painful for some men. A pregnant spouse can be so wrapped up in her own health and the preparations for the baby that she temporarily neglects her partner. That's understandable. Her partner must realize that the baby's arrival is an invitation to grow in love. Without this awareness, emotional immaturity will prevail.

It doesn't matter if your colleague is trying to start an affair. It's your values that are important. So far you have been present, curious and self-disciplined. Be grateful for your integrity. Continue taking steps to avoid becoming involved. This friendship may feel special, but it just complicates his relationship with his wife and with you. He is married, he's not separated, and he's not headed toward divorce. If he tries to flirt, call him on it. Like this: "What would your wife think if she heard you say that to me?" Or: "You might be lonely now, but if we were involved, that loneliness would be replaced by guilt, regret and fear with occasional fireballs of exhilaration. Is it worth it? I don't think so." Show him this kind of backbone, and he will be in awe of you. Yes, that means he will either back away nervously or grow in respect. Either way, you've done the right thing.

Dear Joey,

How do I behave toward all of the people who knew my husband was cheating on me but did nothing about it? They didn't bother to tell me or to talk him out of his affair. Most of them treat me like a pitiful person, but a few seem to be avoiding me altogether. I am so disgusted by their silence, especially because these are supposedly Christians who believe in marriage. What should I do?

Accept their limited understanding of love. Most people think of a wedding as a grand old party. But being a wedding guest is akin to saying yes to sharing responsibility for the spiritual life of the couple. So while the pair pledges faithfulness, the community promises to support that oath. Yes, that means your friends and neighbors were responsible for guiding your husband back to sanity. It also means that a few of them should have had the backbone to tell him he had 48 hours to inform you or they would. Instead, your friends and neighbors chose to mind their own business. Or did they?

Behavior that harms the community is our business. The belief that we should not be involved in the lives of others is an overreaction to the fear of conflict. Investing in another person's life story should never create fear or oppression. And it doesn't when we continually do the inner work that cleans out our own hypocrisy. A true friend would have engaged in the delicate task of helping your husband edit his ego and return to love. The process would have given both individuals a greater sense of their own humanity.

It's painful to discover that you are the last to know something that so deeply impacts every aspect of your life. It's devastating to realize that you have been betrayed by the spouse who vowed to love you and by the community that gathered to care for you. You may not yet be ready for the light in the darkness, but here it is: How wonderful it is to know the truth. People are imperfect. Few can see where their need to control, manipulate and appear "good" infects their words or actions. Forgive them. You are free now to make choices that can lead you to greater peace and joy. Do it and be glad.

Dear Joey,

I was in a four-year relationship until I caught my girlfriend with one of her married co-workers. After months of not speaking to each other, she admitted to me that she had been unfaithful to me for a long time. Now she works in my office. We don't talk or look at each other. I need help handling this situation.

Stop pretending you know her. Her betrayal is proof that she is not who you thought she was. You dated for four years, and she is still a stranger. Treat her accordingly. Say hello politely when your paths cross. If you overhear a rousing conversation between her and a co-worker you like, ignore it. If someone says, "I hear you and (her name here) used to hang out," answer, "Really? What else are people saying?" Then smile. Instead of confirming details, admit, "That was a different lifetime," and exit the conversation. Don't allow anything to distract you from excelling on the job. When your mind floats toward her, rein it back in. Laser-focus on tasks that require your attention, especially career-related issues you procrastinate on. Eventually, the anxiety of what she might do or say will erode. You will no longer care about her presence at work. The payoff for redirecting energy you formerly spent on your now ex-girlfriend will be stellar reviews of your work. And that's an inspiration.

Dear Joey,

My husband cheated and got some woman in his office pregnant. I am proceeding with a divorce. He plans to take a job transfer out-of-state with her. I know this man. He will disappear on me because that's what he did with his former wife when I got pregnant. My problem is our son attends a university that I cannot afford on my own. I need to tell him that he cannot continue. How can I do this? What can I say to my son so he understands?

The truth. But when he learns that his parents are not who he thought they were and that his future is not heading in the direction he imagined, expect explosions. His world has come to an end. Your son will be angry, hurt and likely collapse into a depression, temporarily. You cannot save him from his feelings; do not try. These emotions are expressions of grief and need to be aired and experienced. If your discomfort with his reaction is excessive, he will take care of you and stop tending to himself. That delays the healing process, and his growth may be affected for years, even decades. So don't put your own needs for reassurance above his. It will be important for him to receive counseling during the remainder of this school year. Help him to access a counselor on campus. You will need a network of support, too, and your son should not be a part of it. Do not rely on him to soothe you. It's your job to ensure that his transition is as natural as possible.

Returning to intimacy...

It is possible for a couple to surmount any crisis, including infidelity. All couples, whether dating, cohabitating or married, face calamities in the course of their lives together. Crisis reveals the strengths and weaknesses in the relationship and in each member of the couple. If you want to weather the storm of betrayal, and are committed to moving forward together, follow these steps:

Gather Information: After the discovery of an affair, it's normal to thrash beneath a tsunami of emotions. To move toward the restoration of balance, engage the analytical mind. This is not an attempt to ignore or stuff emotions but rather to include all of ourselves in the process of healing (not just the emotional self). So roll up your sleeves and mindfully gather financial, spiritual and psychological data about the potential outcomes from your choices: staying together, breaking up, securing separate residences until everything is worked out, pursuing legal separation, or getting a divorce. Weigh the options without fear. Prayerfully discern the right path.

Box Up the Blame Game: Blaming is a form of denial that harms everyone. Don't blame and don't shame your partner or yourself. Pour the negative energy of blaming into the positive action of taking responsibility for moving forward into a new chapter of your lives.

Reconnect as a Couple: Find ways to play, flirt and engage in community service as a couple. Remember what you first loved about each other, and stir the ashes and embers of those original memories until the flame of passion returns.

Opt Out of Self-Destructive Behavior: If you notice recurring feelings of guilt or shame, pay attention. Guilt means you think you did a bad thing. Shame means you think you are a bad person. These feelings arise when you are uncertain of the value of staying together, given the possibility of another betrayal. Or when you wonder why you selfishly chose to have an affair and harm your partner. The bottom line is that guilt and shame are signals that you need a neutral third party, like a gifted psychologist, to help you sort things out. Without intervention, it is possible that one or both of you may begin other secret behaviors: a retaliatory affair, excessive drinking or spending money, for example, to attempt to numb the negative feelings.

Look Forward, Together: Any potential problems on the horizon? Name the possible issues and, working as a team, brainstorm solutions. Choose one solution and implement it together. Solving problems before they occur will rebuild your friendship and sense of capability as a couple.

Reconstructing your commitment to one another requires focus, effort and the willingness to grow in love of self and other. It is a spiritual undertaking of the highest order with the capacity to transform every relationship in your life. But take great care not to fall into unhealthy patterns (the affair-addict in a relationship with the co-dependent martyr, for example). Forgiving a betrayal and remaining together is not a more loving choice than forgiving a betrayal and breaking up. The two choices are just different life paths. The key is determining which one is right for you.

3.

Missing in Action

When a date disappears,
it wasn't magic...

Why date? Answer that question for yourself and discover freedom. Some people date for fun, others for status, most to find a life partner, and a few to grow in self-understanding. When you clarify your motivation, it's easier to appreciate every dating experience, even the unexpected disappearance of someone you'd hoped would be your life partner.

Here's how this process works: Let's pretend that you believe the purpose of dating is to find a spouse. That means you expect any series of wonderful dates to lead into an exclusive dating relationship. So what happens when your expectation is not met, and your date stops calling, stops asking you out, or starts refusing your invitations? Inner conflict, confusion and a desperate search for answers, usually. Oh, and a lot of weepy conversations with friends. Plus, there's the pain of banging around in your own head wondering whether to attempt contact one last time with Mr. or Ms. Seemed-So-Right. Or maybe your creative juices flow into imaginative stories, like: "I bet his phone crashed and he lost all of his contacts. That's why he hasn't called." Or: "She's super busy and swamped with work, but I'll hear from her in a few weeks when her schedule opens up." Be honest. If you were super swamped or even without a cell phone, would you prioritize a phone call to someone who has inspired, intrigued and thrilled you? Yes, of course, you would. We always make time for whatever is most important. So don't force yourself to be in the life of anyone who doesn't appreciate who you are and what you bring to his or her life. If you tried to sell someone on believing that you are his or her ideal partner, ask yourself: Did it work? Of course not! There's no need—ever—to sell anyone on how wonderful you are. Anyone who is unable to see you through the eyes of their own heart is not right for you. Ditto that if your love interest disappeared after a few amazing dates.

Dear Joey,

I had two perfect dates with a guy and then never heard from him again, even though he said he would call. We laughed, talked long into the night, he kissed me on the cheek, and asked if I wanted to go out again. It's been two weeks. Should I call him? Or forget about it? What happened?

Life or death, probably. Life: His career has been demanding and exhausting, or he's head over heels for someone else, or a family member is in trouble, and it's all his heart can handle right now. Death: He met someone else and didn't believe he had enough history with you to tell you, or he is afraid to get romantically involved again because at some level he's still nursing the last breakup, or he was just keeping his options open when he said he wanted to see you again, and he didn't actually mean it. In other words, life means his energy is directed elsewhere. Death means that he let go.

Of course, none of these potential storylines are that important, except to our imaginations. But this is: Now you know what a perfect date feels like to you. Pay attention to the details of how you felt and why you felt that way. Put it all in play the next time you are dating, and let it guide you to the right relationship. But don't expend your life energy trying to figure out why two dates didn't transform into a twosome. Just accept the lesson and move forward into your future.

Dear Joey,

I have been dating a guy for three months. Early on, we became close and called each other several times a day. Last week, he stopped returning my calls. He rarely answered the phone and hardly talked when I reached him. Short of showing up at his house, which I considered, I don't know how to find out what is going on. I thought he was "The One," but now he won't talk to me. What is going on?

Your unhealthy ego whispers that you have been abandoned, and that fear ignites your inner stalker. Any behavior outside of an established pattern—like the sudden loss of a phone call that tucks you into bed nightly—startles the ego. The wounded part of the ego obsesses in an attempt to understand what happened, even when it is impossible to understand (our limited perspective stunts our grasp of reality). The healed part of our ego trusts in our own goodness. It pours energy into divesting itself of focus on the other and back into our own lives. But don't just hit the gym more or spend longer hours at work. Instead, give your love to the world through random acts of kindness while expecting nothing in return.

One last thing, romantic ideals like "The One" or "soulmates" are seductive to the neurotic or unhealthy ego but have little to do with a spiritual life. It's difficult to wrap the mind around that kind of truth in a culture corrupted by illusion. But when you shake off false idols, you are free to really love and be loved.

Dear Joey,

I met a man on an online dating site, and after a few emails, we chatted by phone. Later, when we met in person, we talked for over three hours. We hugged before parting, and he said that he'd like to get to know me better. He suggested a movie for the following weekend. I agreed. Well, I didn't hear from him all week. On Saturday, I called and left a message saying that I was looking forward to getting together. It's been two weeks and he hasn't called. I wanted to call him again, but a friend said not to. What's the spiritual message to me in this experience?

Savor the joy of those moments of connection without an expectation that it should lead somewhere. After any delicious date, it's so easy for our minds to concoct stories of a future featuring our new love interest. But if we take these illusions seriously, we suffer. Yes, that's true even if the possibility of another date was dangled before us.

For me, every goodbye is a paradox: closure and continuation. I may never see that friend again, and I will always carry him or her in my heart. Interested in that approach? Try this: Close your eyes. See yourself hugging your date goodbye. Feel the emotions that arise. Now imagine pulling back to observe yourself embracing this man. Notice the thoughts you have about the connection between the two of you and where it might go. Visualize each of these thoughts as a balloon. Acknowledge how you can give yourself everything you wanted from him. Allow those balloons to float away, leaving you clear and free.

Yes, that means don't call this man if you want something from him like an explanation about why he disappeared or whether he wants to go on another date. It may be that he simply changed his mind. Unfortunately, we tend to call people who act this way "flakey," or we accuse them of carelessly hurting someone else's feelings. So rather than admitting the truth ("I'm no longer interested ...") people tend to disappear.

Dear Joey,

I was involved with a woman, but she moved back East. I haven't heard from her, and this is something new for me. I've gotten one card since she's moved and no phone calls. Please help me.

If you've received one card from her, then you have heard from her—just not as much as you'd like. Therein lies the pain. Buddhism describes four kinds of suffering: not getting what you want; getting what you want and not being satisfied by it; being separated from those or that which you love; having to endure the company of those or that which you do not love.

Ready to heal? Make a list of what you miss about the woman you dated. Can you see that you contain all that you seek? Give life to these new parts of yourself by noticing when you embody them. When you do, praise yourself. Your relationship with your former love interest is complete for now, but the connection with yourself is just beginning.

Dear Joey,

I have been eating my heart out over a man I met a few months ago at a club. He called daily until I agreed to go out with him. After we became intimate, he wanted to spend every evening together. He sent me roses and said he was falling madly in love. I felt it, too! We began planning our future. After five weeks of this bliss, he went camping with friends (I had to work). When my schedule changed so I could meet him, he said his ex-wife was there. I didn't go (he says he's not interested in his ex, but you never know). He returned a different man—unhappy with his career and only wanting to see me on weekends. It was true that I had been spending too much time with him, but I felt so betrayed! I want everything the way it was, but he never calls unless he's calling me back, and he never says he loves me. I can't figure out if he ever did love me or if he was just playing me. I cry myself to sleep trying to figure out what I did wrong. I've lost 21 pounds in two weeks. I don't need to lose anymore. Should I just leave him alone?

My sweet friend, leave yourself alone—stop second-guessing your actions. How is it possible that you did anything wrong? You made your choices, and you followed them. You cannot control the actions of another person. He is doing what he's doing, and it has nothing to do with you. So don't try to find fault with yourself. To do so is to rub salt in your wound.

If he said he loved you, trust that that was his truth in that moment. The difficulty is that sometimes people love from their ego when we hope for their souls. The ego's love is fleeting; the soul's is eternal. We can only get to the soul by doing the hard work (or having the difficult experiences) necessary to understand our egos and their shadowy tendencies. Once we gain this understanding, we are less likely to be driven by our egos and more capable of loving compassionately and unconditionally, i.e. from the soul.

Stop wishing for the past. Instead, mail yourself love letters. Send yourself roses. Go to dinner with good friends. Call your own voice mail and leave yourself messages about how radiant you are and what a blessing you are to this world. Heck, leave inspiring sticky notes all over the house! And be generous: Give yourself time to heal.

Dear Joey,

I dated a guy for six months, and in the heat of the moment I asked him to marry me. I have not heard from him since. He has not returned my phone calls or responded to my notes. It's been three weeks. What should I do? There are other guys interested in me, but I don't know what to say to them.

To the guys interested in you: "I just got out of an intense relationship, and I need a little time for reflection before dating again. I will call you in a month or so. If you're still interested, and I hope you will be, we can go out." Note to self: Don't worry about losing any of the guys who are asking you out. Living in that fear is a distraction from what's really important, which is developing self-awareness so you can avoid duplicating mistakes in life.

Second note to self: Don't propose or say, "I love you," for the first time in the heat of the moment, if "heat" is a euphemism for sex or the cuddle segment after. Great sex stimulates every cell in our body into an emotional high that some people confuse with love (it's actually just a great orgasm). If you're in love, the first time you tell your partner should be outside of sexual activity. Saying "I love you" during sex is not romantic, it's a bad cliché. Sex is not love, and love is not sex.

Last note to self: A guy who freaks when offered an open heart, then refuses to communicate with you is not a candidate for any committed relationship. It doesn't matter if he is afraid of hurting your feelings by saying, "No way!" or if he thinks you're psycho because to him the relationship was casual or if he is afraid of repeating his parents' mistakes. The reality is this: He doesn't care enough to tell the truth about his thoughts and feelings. That means he is not a candidate for marriage, which requires truth, trust, mutual caring, commitment and genuine love. P.S. Don't believe that you ruined everything by blurting out a proposal; just admit that he is not the right guy for you.

Dear Joey,

I have a telepathic connection with a man I met a year ago. Although I know I'm a psychic, we've tested our telepathy. My problem is that he won't see me, has moved across town, and is depressed about the end of his marriage. He never calls and is formal in our email messages. He mourns the loss of his wife. I mourn him. I know that when a man does not want you, you should get over him. But we are destined to be together. We left our marriages for the same reasons, were both molested as children, and our hearts have the same kind of wounds. How should I approach a man like this? Should I follow that book, "The Rules," and not get too personal with him or even totally avoid him?

Should you follow "The Rules"? Translation: "Should I try to manipulate him?" Aye-yi-yi! Do you like to be manipulated? Why not just be yourself? Then you can love him as he is, rather than try to force him to include you in his life. If you think that you need him because you believe that you are "destined to be together," you're simply deepening your wound. You can pretend that you've been abandoned and live that drama. Or you can see that something has died and just let it go.

I also suggest that you forget the psychic mind-play. Right now you're using it to help you believe that you know something about your friend. That insistence prevents you from ever really experiencing him. It's being used as a control game, not as a gift. Spirituality is the willingness to not know anything about another person and allow each encounter to unfold anew. Why not try it?

Dear Joey,

I've been emailing a guy in L.A. whom I met on the Internet. I have high moral standards and feel that the guy should always call the girl first, so when he sent his phone number, I didn't call. Eventually I gave him my number, and he left a message. I called a day later and got the distinct feeling that he didn't want to talk. After that, it was email only. He wrote that Valentine's Day "sucked" because he had no one to share it with. I wrote that I expected to be in L.A. soon and maybe we could meet. I haven't heard from him since. My heart says to ignore his future emails and call him in two weeks. Maybe I should also forget about going to L.A. because I'll be tempted to call. I'm not a bad looking woman, and I know I could find somebody else, but there is something about this guy that keeps me hanging on. Normally I would never bother with Internet dating, but my other option is being at the mercy of friends setting me up. What should I do?

Think of email as a digital phone call. So if you sent the first email, you already compromised those "high moral standards." But don't you actually mean high expectations of courtship, not high moral standards? After all, what moral value exists in expecting the man to phone first but then chasing him when he doesn't respond to your advances? Long-term, committed, loving relationships are based in mutuality. If you're not awake to his resistance, you may attempt to win him over by trying to sell him on how wonderful you are. Believe me, that kind of behavior quickly degrades into desperation. Yours. If your relationship pattern is to chase men who avoid emotional intimacy with you, this guy's come-hither-go-to-hell behavior will keep you intrigued, but never content. And that's why you should let go. Next time, remember: 1. In the digital dating world, men offer their phone numbers first as a courtesy. 2. If you get "distinct feelings," be honest and ask if they're true. 3. Don't plan strategies (ignoring email, calling in two weeks) that nurture drama (yes, like the kind you're having right now).

Trust what is…

The desire to love more fully calls us into relationships. But the expectation that a series of dates should lead to a greater commitment inspires drama when it doesn't happen. Why not simply see that series of perfect dates as an education about what a perfect date feels like to you? Detach the experience from the person you dated, and embrace a new level of self-knowledge. By opening your mind to greater possibilities, you are opening your heart to love in a more expansive and generous way.

Be conscious, too, of the ways you may have tried to rush the relationship. While dating, did you push for exclusivity? While exclusive, did you push for sex, living together or marriage? Trying to hurry a relationship along, instead of allowing it time to unfold naturally, can harm your relationship long-term. A relationship that has not proceeded through the necessary markers of maturity—the development of friendship, trust and commitment—will not last. Chemistry alone is not enough.

If you believe in a loving universe, then you know that not hearing back from your former love interest could be the best situation for both of you. Yes, that means the universe might be protecting you from someone you no longer need in your life. It's time to open your eyes. Another treasure is waiting to be discovered. Yes, I mean a newly awakened you. Enjoy!

4.

Moving On

Cling at your own risk...

One of the most painful aspects of a breakup is the sudden change in the rhythm of contact. The "Morning, sweetie!" texts, phone calls during the workday, the ritual of preparing dinner together, movie nights snuggling on the couch—these ritual intimacies are swept away. In the absence of these moments is an ache. If you want it to stop, practice this counterintuitive medicine: Lean into the ache and let it move through you. Don't sit in it. And don't become attached to the belief that what you had in the past is what you should have in the present. Craving what we have lost is a recipe for suffering. Cling at your own risk.

If you are committed to healing and moving on, you must fill the emptiness with something new. Reach out to someone who you know needs attention and give that person your love. Yes, send a "Good Morning" text to a friend or relative. Volunteer at a soup kitchen, or invite a neighbor to make dinner with you. Snuggle on the couch alone until you can fall in love with solitude and the pleasure of your own company.

As your grieving nears completion, take charge of your mind. If a memory arises, let it pass through you. Observe your thoughts and emotions, but don't allow yourself to get stuck in any of it. Engage your ability to thrive with curiosity and compassion for yourself. Refuse to believe any thought your mind presents that causes fear. Insist on the perfection of even this experience. Eventually, you will discover that moving forward is an act of love, for yourself and for everyone who looks to you to learn how to live fully on this beautiful planet.

Dear Joey,

My five-year relationship ended last summer. He was the first person I ever loved, and I considered him my best friend and family. Now he won't talk to me. I am sad and still cry whenever I think about him and the times we had together. I think he's pretty much forgotten me. How do people move on?

By accepting the truth: The relationship is not damaged, it's over. After a breakup, many people avoid what they most need to hear: the truth. So here's another serving: Stop living in the past. Yes, your heart aches. That's understandable. Yes, you are mourning the loss of an important person in your life and your hopes for a shared future. I get it. But if you continue to allow nostalgia to infect you, expect pain. The heart hurts whenever the mind invests in the past, the body resides in the present, and there's a failure to believe in a future.

Grieving the demise of a relationship is normal. But don't use memories to elicit tears and drive yourself deeper into melancholy. And if you prolong your pain with self-blame ("If I was different… I should have done…"), please stop. It's an addictive pattern that wastes energy. Redirect your attention into gleaning lessons from this relationship so you can make better choices in the future. Here's a tutorial: Widen your concept of family. Choosing one person to be your entire support system is a recipe for co-dependency. Another lesson: If you have one best friend, that's a blessing. If you fail to commit yourself to other friendships because you're overly attached to your best friend, that's a problem. A final lesson: When a former partner refuses to talk to you, consider why. Perhaps, after the break-up, your need for reassurance coiled beneath every word you spoke. If so, your ex-boyfriend extricated himself because he wanted protection from your neediness. The end of a relationship requires that we accept responsibility for ourselves; interdependence is over.

Move on by going to therapy while also devoting yourself to new and old friendships (this means you learn about your friends and share about yourself, but do not drag out the carcass of your relationship for a show-and-tell of suffering every time someone asks how you are). No friends? Take classes, volunteer, vacation, visit relatives, go to a 12-step meeting, clean your closets, go on a supervised retreat, make a list of the things you always wanted to try and then try them. Um, did I mention therapy? It can teach you to be a better friend to yourself.

Dear Joey,

I met and fell in love with a wonderful man. One weekend, we went to Lake Tahoe to celebrate his birthday, and for some reason we didn't connect. He used that weekend as the reason to break up with me. He admits that the year we spent together was good but said that our Tahoe weekend proved that we did not get along. He refused to work it out. I can't forget him. What do you suggest?

Concentrate on remembering you. By transferring attention back "home," you might discover that you're really in love with the you who was in an intimate relationship with him. Perhaps that version of you felt more sensual or attractive or intelligent or loving or funny (or whatever) than ever before. If so, it's important to understand that you don't need this man in order to be a new, more expansive self. Although the experience of this relationship may have awakened you, the power to be that self exists completely in you.

Consider why you allow your history to be more important than the reality of now. Giving an emphasis to the past perpetuates a sense of imbalance (just like overemphasizing the present or future). Maintaining a balance between the past, present and what is to come, invites you into the stability that you seek. Be certain, too, that your love for this friend (or anyone) is at least equal to your love for yourself. Otherwise, you are simply creating a false idol, a man-god to distract you from the work of creating the best life for yourself.

Dear Joey,

I've been dating a former professor of mine. I told him I wanted to get serious by having a casual but monogamous relationship with him. He got upset at me for expressing my feelings and backed off. He doesn't even call anymore. When I bump into him at school, he pretends everything is A-OK. It seems like he needs his space to think about things. Should I continue talking to him or give him his space?

Honey, you can't give him space. You can't give someone something that he or she already owns. Focus instead on confronting the mental clutter in your own head that prevents you from seeing the relationship as it is. So when you see him, pay attention to how you feel and what you are thinking. Notice any thoughts arising that are fearful or unkind. Choose not to act on these. Realize that, for him, everything is fine, as is. Let that be okay for you, too. And, when you encounter this man on campus, say hello in a kind and friendly way and keep on walking. Do not attempt to chat, flirt or otherwise solicit attention from him. Live in reality: You are no longer in a relationship.

Dear Joey,

My fiancé left me last year claiming that she did not get enough attention, sexually and otherwise. I could not sleep, eat, or function properly at work. I lost my job. When we first met, she had just divorced an abusive man. I treated her like a goddess compared to him. She left me for an abusive man and would call me, crying. She refused to leave him. She said she had nowhere to go and would not live with me because I live in a motel. I just want to know if I am capable of loving again.

My magic 8-ball says, "Of course!" The real question to ask yourself, though, is this: Was it love? You were emotionally involved with a woman who was not emotionally available. That inspires feelings of longing, melancholy and neediness, all of which fuel infatuation, lust and drama. This passes for love, but it's just an illusion. Genuine love is steady, secure, even boring at times, and certainly not saturated with drama. So grieve the end of the relationship and the death of the illusion that it was true love. Then gain the support necessary to be emotionally sober so that you can be available for the real thing.

Dear Joey,

I met a woman at a singles party last year. We hit it off right away and seemed to have a lot in common. She lives in the Bay Area, so basically we were spending weekends together getting to know each other. We were really attracted to each other and got involved physically right away. I invited her to join me recently on a vacation I had already planned to Cancun. It seemed like the perfect location for romance, but she flipped out. It was like she was a different person altogether, moody and complaining about everything. It seemed like nothing I did was right. Then she began talking about her ex-husband and how she wished he was dead. This is a beautiful, church-going woman! I suggested that she fly back early and alone. Then I hung out by myself to try and figure out how a perfect romance went haywire. Any ideas?

Shrink your dating pool. When you date someone in, or close to, your own ZIP code, you have a better opportunity to see how she really lives, works and plays. If your romantic interest lives more than an hour away, each date can feel like a honeymoon. Those five days of "I miss you so much!" build up expectations and sexual tension. By the time you actually meet in person, the encounter is slathered in romance but not much substance. And since both people are presenting their "best" selves, it may be impossible to discover that you have few common interests or completely different values, or that he or she has no conflict resolution skills until after your body tells you that the great sex you're having with this person means that she or he is "The One."

Long-distance or short, the healthy way to begin any romance is as friends. That's not an anthem against sex but rather a respect for it—and for our hearts. When a relationship turns physical too soon, we become committed to someone we barely know and who we sometimes later lament should be committed (to prison or mental health treatment or hell!). The real problem, though, was that we didn't take the time to take care of ourselves in the beginning by learning about the person's character before surrendering to our hormones. So the next time you are tempted to begin a romantic relationship, keep your mind and body from arguing with each other by starting that relationship off on the solid foundation of friendship.

Dear Joey,

How can I overcome loneliness? I ended a relationship over a year ago because we were not on the same spiritual plane, although the relationship was good on many levels. It was the right decision, yet my heart yearns for him. Well, I'm not sure if it's him or the companionship that I miss, although I have no desire to rekindle our relationship. I have some good friends (male and female), a strong commitment to God, and a busy social calendar, but I long for the day I won't be plagued with loss.

To be a spiritual person is to live what is learned from spiritual experiences, those spontaneous moments when you understand the paradox of being simultaneously a unique individual and in union with all. These experiences teach us to hold our beliefs lightly. So if someone else doesn't share your beliefs about, say, reincarnation, it's not a reason to disengage from the relationship or even to lessen your respect for him or her. This is because you love your individuality and his enough to let each of you be who you are. But if you wanted him to be more like you (aka, less like himself) by adhering to the beliefs you favored, that's kin to starting a personal religion. This doesn't mean that you shouldn't have a loved one or even a circle of support that enjoys beliefs that are similar to yours. Just notice if you thought, "My life would be better if he ...," and if that idea inspired you to end the relationship before it had a natural death through the blossoming of your own growth, not the forced fertilization of his.

When the thought, "I'm lonely," arises, slow yourself down. Otherwise, you might cascade into pools of sadness and despair. Ask yourself if you are truly lonely or if you are simply recognizing that you are alone. If you insist on "alone," ask yourself whether such a thing is possible on this planet. If you live the awareness offered in a spiritual experience of union, you understand that you are connected to all that is, so you are never really alone. If you really possess "a strong commitment to God," then being lonely is impossible. God is always with you. So unwrap the lie of loneliness. You'll build the strength necessary to find peace in any experience.

Dear Joey,

My boyfriend and I broke up last year when I discovered that he was sweet on his boss. Five months later, he asked for a second chance. We agreed to take commitment slowly because we love each other. All was well until he lost his job. He slid into a depression, and I rescued him with my time and money. He seemed to appreciate and want me around. Then he became distant and would not make love to me. I discovered that he was using cocaine and staying up all night masturbating to porn. I love him and want to save our intimacy and regard for each other. Last weekend when I asked how I could help our sex life, he said, "I guess watching me f*** another girl is out of the question." He later apologized. But now his former boss has her own company and wants to hire him. I don't want to watch him pursue her. So yet another relationship ends with my partner choosing someone else and leaving me by the wayside. I don't know what to do. I love him, but he lives two hours away and says that four years is too soon for us to consider engagement or marriage.

If you dated this man for forty years, it would be the same story. That's because he is addicted to distracting himself (cocaine, pornography, other women) from fully engaging in a relationship that is emotionally, spiritually, mentally and physically intimate. You are addicted to him. Why? Well, a relationship with him allows you to perpetuate your habit: recreating the pattern in which a partner abandons you for someone else. What debilitating belief about yourself do you get to maintain by continuing to resuscitate that pattern?

I believe that your relationship is an abusive one. Where is the love? Of you by you, I mean. Can you see how you choose to leave yourself by the wayside, giving all you have to a man and accepting less in return? How committed are you to closure of this experience?

A wise professor of theology once said, "All beginnings and endings are mythological." In other words, the Divine is calling you toward something greater: a larger understanding of yourself and your place in the world. An extended period of solitude would allow the insight needed to discover how you make choices that invite betrayal.

Dear Joey,

My boyfriend's friends have sex with different girls every week, and my boyfriend feels like he is missing out. He's 21 years old, and our relationship is his first serious one. Before we began dating, he followed me around until we became best friends. I finally fell in love. Everything was perfect for six months, but then he said he stopped loving me and ended our relationship. After two weeks apart, we met and could not stop smiling at each other. He said he missed me, loved me and was just scared that everything was too good. We got back together, but he still thought about leaving me. I know he loves me. He even gave me a ring on New Year's. Now he has ended our relationship again, saying he wants to see how life is without me. He wants to stay friends, but I said I can't because I love him. I know I should forget about him and live my life, but I believe that he'll be back someday. Am I in denial?

Worrying about whether you're in denial just puts one more layer between you and reality. That's more complication than a suffering mind needs. Instead, focus on the truth: It doesn't matter whether this man will be back someday or not. The reality is he's not here now. Inspired by that knowledge, how do you choose to live your life? I don't suggest continuing the lady-in-waiting routine. Why put your romantic life on hold for a man who is so certain that having sex with a different woman every week makes life worth living? What could possibly motivate you to give yourself completely to a man who is willing to give himself up to multiple opportunities to score STDs? Don't say "love," unless you mean the love of drama. You may have an affection for each other, but genuine love is deep, abiding and does not drive a person to drop a committed relationship in order to fulfill random sexual urges or the admiration of his buddies.

The problem, of course, is not that your former boyfriend has had few relationships. The difficulty is that he's immature emotionally, mentally and spiritually. His age is not the culprit. Lack of self-knowledge, self-esteem and self-awareness is. He doesn't have the self-confidence to be himself; he needs to belong to a group of guys who would rather put their health and true happiness at risk than experience real intimacy. That doesn't make him a bad guy, just a terribly superficial, confused and manipulative one. And that explains why you've been on an emotional rollercoaster. Your feelings are not signs of love's highs and lows, they're signs of chaos. Love yourself enough to see the end of this relationship as an opportunity to have a healthy commitment with someone capable of it.

Dear Joey,

I did everything to make my relationship work. I accepted that at times I wouldn't get what I wanted and would go elsewhere (depending on the experience I felt was missing) or do without and be as present as possible with what was between my girlfriend and me. Still, we broke up. I feel as if I gave too much or that what I gave wasn't enough. I think I used the relationship to develop a sense of direction in my life. It often happens that I don't know what I've been using a person for until well after the fact. Is it better to be up front with others about why I am in a relationship with them, or is this an awareness that I keep to myself?

There is no rule to guarantee the safety of your heart. But there are general principles to guide you through the thicket or fruit of relationships. The first is: Know yourself. If your self-understanding is deep, your ability to discern how you're using others will be clear. So, yes, delve into your own motivations about why you are in a relationship. Your regrets are guides toward your development of independence, which is a critical juncture leading to interdependence. Be in relationship with each regret, until you learn the story of its birth and how to lay it to rest. Realize, too, that if we are in a relationship to know ourselves, the closure of a relationship is also in service of our wholeness.

Dear Joey,

Until three years ago, I was in a relationship with someone who I thought was my life partner. When she suddenly (and without reason) moved out, my heart was broken. I have been in two relationships since but was not emotionally available, so I recoiled when they became serious. I really believed I would never love again, but I have now fallen in love. I am scared to death of being vulnerable, being known, or making a fool of myself. Could you give me some perspective on how to love and have a meaningful romantic relationship? I need advice before I do something to ruin this.

There is a Buddhist teacher who cautions against falling in love. His refreshing refrain is that we should stand in love. I think that such an image allows us to be grounded and capable for what is surely the true work of our lives. Genuine love involves radical truth, trust, commitment, selfless caring, challenge and risk. So your fears are realistic. You will be vulnerable, known and a fool if you love another really well because you'll risk ruining any mask you've grown comfortable with. So here's some medicine: When fear arises, return to the components of genuine love (truth, etc.), and push yourself to be vulnerable. If you are with the right partner, the experience will draw you both into intimacy and ruin your idea that you could ruin a genuine love relationship.

Dear Joey,

Am I obsessed with my ex? I never considered it before a friend said something, but I talk about him 24/7, go places he might be, and places we went together. I drive home by the route he takes. I call just to hear his voice. I still have the things he gave me, and I torment myself looking at his photo. I feel desperate; I need him to go on. What can I do to help myself?

Stop living under the illusion that the past is more real than the present. If you choose to live in reality—yes, that means life without your ex—the worst thing that can happen is that you'll have to combat your fear of rejection or abandonment. Facing these fears will help you to be healthier in your next relationship. Until then, practice this mantra: I want what God wants for me. It will help you to surrender your will to God's will (also known as reality). And be careful. If you continue stalking your ex, he might file a restraining order against you.

Dear Joey,

Every time my girlfriend of six months and I fight, she changes her Facebook status to single. It pisses me off, and then I panic at the thought of losing her, so I suck it up and apologize. The whole thing makes me so distracted that I can't even do my job. I don't want to get fired, but I'm getting so depressed about always fighting that I just don't really care about much anymore. I read your column all the time, so I know you're going to tell me to break up with her, but I don't think I can.

Oh, honey! Of course you have the skills to end a relationship that is shattering your self-esteem. If you can't have a healthy disagreement without the threat of being kicked to the curb, then it's not much of a relationship anyway. When your girlfriend expresses her post-argument anger by switching her Facebook status to single, she's being passive-aggressive by publicly punishing you. Whatever it triggers inside (yes, from your family history) inspires enough shame to send you groveling back. If you're not ready for a breakup, take an extended break from this relationship rut. The next time you and this woman argue, walk away but offer to return when both of you are capable of real conversation. Then resist checking her Facebook status. Engage your superhero will (we all have it) to resist responding to her. Every time you start to call, text or IM her—stop. Put your phone or computer aside, and handle some work-related task you have been ignoring. That's right. Move the rest of your life forward while your love connection is stuck. If you're totally on top of your "To Do" list, then take a walk around your hood or along the river, but leave your phone at home to avoid temptation. Eventually, you will realize that when you're ready to lay down good boundaries, you won't need to be her doormat.

Dear Joey,

I am middle-aged, single, with a solid profession, good friends and a comfortable home. I pray to meet the man who is my true life partner, but I am afraid to meet him. I have been unsuccessful in past relationships. I rarely meet available men, so when I finally get a date, I am so desperate, I rush into a full-blown relationship with a guy who no one in their right mind would choose. I hang on longer than I should, and then it ends. I'm starting to date again and hope you can help me avoid another psychodrama relationship.

Perhaps the psychodrama relationships are leading you to your true love. Each of us has areas of immaturity as a result of traumas, large and small, in our personal histories. Some people learn to grow beyond these flashpoints within the container of a single, committed partnership. Others manage the same progress through a series of relationships. Of course, growth and subsequent emotional integration doesn't occur automatically. For those who avoid emotional union in a single, committed relationship or those who propel themselves into a relationship immediately after the breakup of another, healing does not occur at all. It comes as the result of engaging in honest reflection following an emotional challenge or after a breakup.

Here's an exercise that can help. Write a one-paragraph description of each "psychodrama relationship" (in historical—not hysterical—order). Then take a break. Go for a walk, or dance around your living room to your favorite tunes. Return to the list. Read each paragraph individually, and respond to it by writing what you gained by being in that relationship and what lessons you learned about yourself. Next, admit whether you have truly integrated this information into your life. If not, write an explanation of why you have not and how you can change in the future. Be honest. This means there will be nothing on your page that blames your ex-boyfriends or otherwise projects your own failures on to them. Focus on yourself. Eventually, if you remain open to possibilities, you will meet someone who is the one you hope for.

Dear Joey,

I am just out of a five-year, long-distance relationship and wondering if I will ever find someone that is right for me.

You just completed a relationship with someone who was right for you for five years. How do I know? I looked at your choice to commit for five years. So your real question is whether you will ever find a life partner. Yes. If you understand that the spiritual purpose of relationship is to help you understand yourself and change until your compassion is as wide as the night sky, then you also understand that the ultimate partner for you is—you. Everyone else who shows up to befriend and romance you is simply present to move you to the next stage of your spiritual evolution. If you are paying attention (and not everyone does), you will learn from every lost opportunity to love then open your heart to become the dynamic, blessed being you are intended to be.

Dear Joey,

I searched for and found an old friend on Facebook. I hadn't heard from her for about 12 years, but we started talking. She told me that she had a boyfriend, but we kept talking anyway. When she flew back here to visit family over the holidays, we went out. She said that she is not happy at all in her relationship. Her boyfriend has cheated on her several times. They live together, and I know that she hasn't left yet because she is comfortable. So do I wait for her to come around, or do I move on? I know that she really likes me, and her mother has also told me this.

Of course she likes you, honey. You're a sweet connection to her past and the hope of a better future. But right now, you are also just a pleasant distraction. She claims to be unhappy with her cheating boyfriend, and you think it's because she is comfortable. Most people who have settled into the rhythm of being betrayed continue the same missteps even after changing partners. So if you get involved, your love interest may have difficulty trusting you. She might express irrational worries about the relationship ending. And, if she's not particularly aware, she might cheat on you, inflicting the pain inflicted on her. Oh, it's possible that she will suddenly be ready for a healthy relationship with you, but don't count on it.

Dear Joey,

I've just dumped another emotionally unavailable guy. Why do I date guys who are not into me?

At the core of your beliefs about yourself is this lie: "I'm unlovable." You're itching to ditch it, but instead of investigating the belief and challenging it, you've opted to search outside yourself for someone to rescue you from it. So you pass through one relationship after another, hoping to find someone who will love you, the prince who will kiss your wound and heal it forever. Instead, you repeat the same relationship pattern because that core belief is still in charge of your choices. If a guy's not into you, it proves you're unlovable. That means you get to be right (your need to be right must be another core belief) and unlovable. I suggest beginning every day with an inventory of all the ways you know you are worthy and loving. Then spend the day falling in love with yourself.

Dear Joey,

My boyfriend and I were getting back together after a month apart. Then he broke up with me again before he left town for New Year's. He said he doesn't want to be a couple anymore. He wants me to be around to talk to because he loves me to death, but cannot handle it when I question him about why he doesn't call me as much, hang out with me, or take me where he goes. He said that he still wants me to call him and all that stuff. He'll be back Saturday, but it is driving me nuts because I do not know what he is doing and who he is with. He trusts me, but I do not trust him. He said he'll call every night, but he doesn't. I feel stupid waiting but think I should to prove that I love him and want to be with him. But I do not feel like he is even trying to save this relationship. After two years, it is hard to let go. What do you think?

I think that you should make friends with reality. Start here: Your romantic relationship is over; there is nothing to save. What he is doing and who he is with is none of your business because your relationship has ended. It's d-e-a-d. Of course, you can try to resuscitate the corpse for a few more weeks or months, but why bother? It just prolongs the pain.

The intensity of your attachment to this man is not a sign of your love; it's a symptom of your addiction to low self-esteem. Who knows why he behaves as he does? It is possible, for example, that he has serious intimacy issues. He avoids committing so he can remain in denial about his real problems. Or he may already be involved with someone else and lacks the cojones to be honest. Regardless of what he is doing, your neediness suffocates your self-confidence. And, honey, that ain't sexy.

Love blossoms when two independent people come together, are truthful about themselves, and gradually learn to trust and depend on each other. Now, that is sexy. So instead of begging him to include you in his life, pinch yourself awake and get a life for yourself. Invest energy into something that would improve your life or the life of others. Become a volunteer, take a class, begin seeing a counselor, or join a Co-Dependent's Anonymous group. Become someone you would never want to leave.

Dear Joey,

After 25 years of marriage, my wife and I separated last year. Despite two fine and healthy sons, a warm and comfortable home, and jobs that challenged and fulfilled us, we were not happy. Our lives and friends changed, we drifted apart, and communication ended. The deaths of family members and friends did not help our situation. I began to see my life as a limited journey. I yearned to grow and complete what I was destined to accomplish, thus our pending divorce. While separated, I have been able to produce some of the best artwork of my career. I also became involved with a young art student. Our relationship was great for six months, until I found myself weaving the same communication pattern in my relationship with her as I did in my marriage. We have since parted friends, but I am left wondering what lesson I need to learn to prevent this from happening again. I can almost hear you telling me to first love my "Art God" and then center myself. I think I do, but I have a hard time communicating with those I love. Please offer advice.

An artist I know says, "You must be yourself when you make art, and even if you don't want to reveal yourself, you are." The same is true of good communication. You must allow your authentic self to shine through and then listen deeply as another does the same. The result is like experiencing inspired art; you are forever transformed because your entire body has witnessed and felt revelation.

The key, of course, is a willingness to reveal yourself. Sometimes we withhold our thoughts, defending against the possibility of criticism. The paradox is that the more we tell the truth about ourselves, the less we can be hurt. It's like that old Meredith Brooks song where she sings, "I'm a bitch, I'm a lover, I'm a mother ..." If I tell you I'm sometimes a bitch, what power do you have over me when you call me one? Telling the truth about myself means that I can unplug from a potential argument by softening to admit, "Yes, I am a bitch, sometimes. I'm working on it and I'm sorry that I hurt you."

One more thing: Take care with the thought that your artistic breakthrough is connected to your separation. It may be. But sift through the past months, and see if there are other reasons. Otherwise, you may find yourself subconsciously creating a pattern in which you manufacture a reason to leave a relationship so that you can be free to produce art you admire.

Dear Joey,

I separated from my wife after she cheated on me. Our divorce is underway. Since I moved out two months ago, I met an amazing woman and can imagine spending the rest of my life with her. I know this sounds sudden, but really, we click in ways I never dreamed possible and never had with my wife. The problem is that I find myself holding back in this new relationship. I struggle with feeling inadequate and obsess about my wife's affair (it was with a family friend). Do you have any suggestions for how I can get through this and enjoy the opportunity I have for real happiness with my true love?

Divest your brain of the notion that your new romantic interest is a ticket to paradise. Maybe she is, maybe not. But casting her in the role of savior dumps a payload of expectation on her and on the relationship. Do you understand what that means? You have sentenced yourself to endless feelings of inadequacy. After all, it's impossible to feel equal to someone whose job it is to save you from yourself.

An extramarital affair is a deeply painful betrayal. Your mind darts through memories, seeking the moment your spouse's heart slipped away. You wonder how you missed that moment and whether bad luck is a permanent construct of your personality. All of these fears (and more) are normal, but not useful. Ultimately, you must discover what attitudes and behaviors you (not your soon-to-be ex-wife) engaged in that created distance. Focus on experiencing this as homework, a way to delve deeper into becoming a more honest version of you. Once completed, holding back is unnecessary. Resistance simply means you have not accomplished the internal work required to be emotionally available. As the delightful Muslim poet Rumi once wrote, "Your task is not to seek for love but merely to seek and find all of the barriers within yourself that you have built against it." Jumping into another committed relationship while your emotional wounds are still oozing is not what the poet had in mind. You need a guide through the thicket of your pain and into another reality. A skilled psychotherapist, a men's group or a 12-step program can help.

The leap of faith...

Remember the scene in the film "Indiana Jones and the Last Crusade" when Indiana Jones is standing on the edge of an enormous chasm? Transit is easy once he embodies faith in a future he cannot see. Indy steps forward and bridges the distance from where he is stuck to where he wants to be. His faith materializes a new reality that allows him to trust that a path will appear. It does.

The same is true for you. Your heart has been broken, your dreams shattered. It feels like the end of the world. In reality, though, you stand on a ledge, at the edge of all possibilities. You can remain stuck in the past. You can stand on the ledge with a closed heart, dreading your new life. Or you can take a leap of faith, trusting that, within you, is everything required for the journey forward into happiness. Afraid? Embody faith in a future that you cannot fully imagine. How? By remembering this: You will love again. You will be loved again. What has happened is part of the experience of being alive because releasing and rising is the rhythm of life. Everything is possible. Have faith in yourself. Take the first step.

5.

Closure

If you've come undone...

Closure is an illusion. There will always be unanswered questions and uncertainty when a relationship ends. Most of the time we feel compelled to wrestle with the unknown. This inspires stress. Instead, when your mind lingers on unanswered questions, resist. Deny the impulse to contact your former partner for reassurance and solutions. Let your mind and heart grow accustomed to living beautifully, despite uncertainty. After all, no answer he or she offers can grant the peace you seek. Inner peace arrives as a result of your willingness to discipline your mind. And, learning to live with mystery, with loose ends and questions, strengthens your capacity to stay centered no matter what happens. You gain a priceless skill: how to live in reality in a world filled with the unknown. Practice trusting that someday, you will understand completely what is necessary to understand about the questions that remain. Until then, be content to practice the art of not knowing. Commit to it as an act of personal devotion. Let it birth in you the trust in yourself that true love of self brings.

Dear Joey,

I need to ask for forgiveness from my former partner. My conscience bothers me, and I am uncomfortable with the way our relationship ended. I have not yet tried to talk with her because I believe I will have just one chance. The idea of forgiveness is very important for me to move on. But I am unsure where she is in regards to the relationship. I would like to address some issues with her before it's too late.

You can't know that you will have just one chance to bring clarity to this situation. The world is wrapped in equal measures of revelation and mystery, so no matter how much you think you know, there will always be moments, even chapters, of your life that remain unpredictable. Believing that you have only one chance adds tension to a situation that you intend to be centered in peace.

There's a chasm between addressing issues with her and asking for forgiveness. Addressing issues is about being right. It can create more friction than it solves. Forgiveness requires that you dive deeply into your own heart and take complete responsibility for whatever you believe that you did to her and for much, if not all, of what you think she did to you. It's clean, simple and holy. It doesn't snivel and it isn't righteous.

If you need her forgiveness in order to move on, you've missed a step in the process. Before asking for forgiveness or apologizing in any way, you must do the inner work necessary to forgive yourself. If nothing else, you can forgive yourself because the behavior that you engaged in is what you knew to do at the time (that's why you did it), and it has made you the person you are now (a bit wiser). In this way, forgiveness remains the gentle sacrament that it is meant to be.

Dear Joey,

I dumped my ex-boyfriend a year ago because he refused to get married. I just attended a holiday party and found out that he is engaged with plans to get married in February. I am completely broken up over this. I am too distracted to be a good friend. I keep wondering if there is something wrong with me. Please help.

There is nothing wrong with you, honey. He just wasn't the one for you. So really allow yourself to enjoy the single life and its many pleasures. Learn to appreciate solitude, revel in the joy of a household arranged to your liking, and be grateful for the freedom to make plans without consulting anyone. That way, when you do marry, you can immerse yourself in that new delight without regret.

Although you don't say so directly, it appears that you think you were betrayed by your ex-boyfriend's choice. Could you also have betrayed yourself by giving so much of yourself away? Or by limiting your own dating because you insist he is "The One"? I think you need more honesty in your life.

Practice truthfulness with friends, too, by saying, "I'm really not present in this conversation right now, and I do want to hear what you have to say. Can we be silent a moment while I collect my thoughts?" Or excuse yourself and go to the bathroom, look in the mirror, and call your chattering mind back to the present moment. Then head back to the chat. After all, you might be missing a soul connection during those conversations with friends. And that would be a needless waste of love.

Dear Joey,

I cannot stop thinking about my ex-boyfriend who recently married. I even had a few dreams about him. Can you help me forget and be happy for him?

Yes! He is not the man for you. How do I know? Because he married someone else! When your thoughts drift toward him, rein them in. Refocus on making yourself the ideal partner to the most ideal partner you can imagine for yourself. If you feel overwhelmed by an "Oh-poor-me!" attitude, pray: "Inspire me to move through these feelings with dignity so that I may appreciate all examples of genuine love in the world. Help me to trust that my life is in right order. And may my prayer serve anyone, anywhere, who is in the same situation as I am." Then be grateful for all of the goodness in your life: breath, clean water, friends (keeping adding to the list until happiness bursts from every cell of your body).

Dear Joey,

After ending our relationship, my ex-boyfriend said he still wanted to be "great friends." Although our relationship was plagued by his unwillingness to fully commit, I initially agreed since we have mutual friends. Later, he defined "great friends" as bed buddies without a commitment. I refused, and he became a complete asshole. I'm courteous to him but feel like I'm betraying myself because my rage threatens to swallow me. Am I angry at myself because I let myself be treated this way? Is my anger righteous? How can I work through all of this so that my forgiving nature can be restored?

When you swallow your truth because you want to be seen as nice, you are abandoning yourself. You are being as much of a jerk to yourself as you say that your ex-partner is being to you. After all, doesn't "bed buddies without commitment" define the relationship you two had prior to your breakup? You probably tried to tell yourself as much but refused to listen. Rage is big enough to demand your focus. It's your blessed wake-up call to the ways you abuse yourself and blame others for that abuse. And, yes, that's why you are angry at yourself, your ex, and the world of ideas in your head about what mutual friends might think of you.

Here's your homework assignment: Treasure yourself enough to clear the fear that keeps you from being honest (first to yourself, then others). Remember, your ex-partner is just being the same guy he always was. His behavior says nothing about you. Your goodness cannot be taken from you—not even by you. It's time for you to recognize that. When you do, forgiving yourself will be a snap.

Dear Joey,

My ex-girlfriend sent a nasty email demanding the return of a coat that she left at my house months ago. She was abusive while we dated, and I just want her to treat me with respect. I am also angry about her refusal to reimburse me for airline tickets that she promised to repay. I am angry at myself, too, because when she and I met, she owed money to her previous boyfriend and refused to pay it. I've thought about dumping the coat at Goodwill or requiring her to pick it up. I have started to date someone else, but this situation bothers me.

Forgive the debt. It's tuition for the "Why did I think it would be different with me?" course at the University of Rotten Relationships. Revenge scenarios (dumping the coat) reveal your fear of an imbalance of power: She still has it, you want it. You probably felt this way throughout the relationship, but if you admitted that, you would have left (thus keeping self-respect intact). Attempting to ransom the coat allows you to maintain contact and pretend to be in charge. This fragile connection supports your illusion that she will change and become the woman you imagined her to be (respectful). But hanging on to an unhealthy relationship, waiting for a crumb of positive recognition, is an act of desperation. If you refuse future contact, you refuse opportunities to be manipulated. That raises your self-confidence. It also supports you in being fully present for your new relationship. Box the coat and send it back. Or leave it with the receptionist at her office and jet away.

Dear Joey,

My girlfriend and I broke up, but that's not the problem. We have the same circle of friends, hang out at the same bars, and in general are bound to run into each other repeatedly. Ideas?

Yes, be gracious (rooted in Divine grace and compassion). Smile, say hello, and then move on to other friends. As your comfort grows, engage in casual conversation. If, at any time, you are yearning for her attention or want to warn someone about what she is really like, take a timeout from your shared circle of pals. See a counselor, and get clear about whether those thoughts are about her or if they're really about you. For example, are you afraid of seeing her with someone else? Acknowledge that possibility to yourself, and you'll grow stronger. Be grateful that she found someone new, and look forward to the same for yourself. Remember, if you didn't grow in humility and love during a romantic relationship, the end of that relationship gives you an exquisite chance to expand your capacity to love and be loved.

Dear Joey,

I have a friend whose former relationships were homosexual. I guess he's now bisexual because he fell deeply in love with a young woman (she's 23 and he's 60) and she with him. He says he is devoted to her and can't imagine his life without her, despite the difference in their ages, race, religion (he is an Episcopal priest) and ethnicity. I have told him that I'm happy for him but am cautious, too, because I don't want to see him hurt. Still, I feel guilty. I guess I hoped that if he ever wanted to be with a woman, he might think of me. I am stunned by the hurt and jealousy I feel. I feel like I've lost something that I never had. I'm almost 41 but have no previous experience to help me through this. How can I move through these feelings? I want to celebrate his happiness.

You obviously care deeply for your friend and are generous-hearted enough to want to stretch beyond your disappointment and jealousy. Don't hurry the process. Slow down and try to understand how you inspired the feelings that now disrupt you. For example, you chose to silently harbor romantic fantasies about your friend while accepting that nothing could transpire. By not confronting your feelings (Why am I so interested in someone who is not available to me?), you neglected them. If you haven't been tending your emotions, it's natural to feel cautious while facing a situation that could force self-examination. So although you attached your caution to your friend's news, it's really your defenses that created caution. So let's translate: When you say that you don't want to see your friend hurt, you really mean that you don't want to see yourself hurt. Why? Some people believe that being hurt implies that they were vulnerable, which they believe is negative. But we can't really love another unless we drop our defenses. And, yes, that makes us vulnerable.

I don't think that you should tell your friend that you dreamed of a relationship with him. He's involved with someone else, so your confession would only create drama. I do believe that you should admit to yourself that you desire a loving, committed companion. Treat that desire with tenderness. This will eventually transform those feelings of jealousy and loss into the urge to create the right romantic relationship for you.

Dear Joey,

I expected to marry the girl I dated in college, but we broke up. She said that she would never date a co-worker, but she screwed some guy she works with. I need guidance on forgiving, forgetting and moving on.

I think you'll find it easier to forgive her after you've forgiven yourself. So what could you forgive yourself for? It could be something as subtle as ignoring the sweet voice of your own intuition because you were trying to be nice or make her happy. At some point we have to wake up to the reality that denying ourselves in hopes of making another happy only creates two unhappy people. So search your mind and heart to see where you betrayed yourself. Once you accept your behavior, you'll have no difficulty extending understanding to your ex-girlfriend. The gift in this process is that you'll shift from victim to equal. True communion is accepting oneself as equal to another, rather than pretending powerlessness or attempting mastery. You embody equality when you admit to yourself that you are or have been capable of similar acts. At that point compassion grows in your heart, and you understand that your ex-girlfriend is simply being herself. There is nothing personal in her action, nothing against you. She simply changed her rules and failed to tell you. If you believe that she should have behaved differently, be the model of the behavior you prefer. Expecting anyone else to do so is an invitation to suffering.

As you heal, take care not to concoct stories about her based on suspicion and gossip. Focusing on her life, rather than your own, will only distract you. After you've gleaned all possible wisdom from this experience, you'll forget it. And if you've read this far, you're already moving on.

Dear Joey,

My ex-boyfriend wants to get back together, but the reason we broke up was that I could not trust him. He says he's changed. But he was so secretive before, about everything, that I never felt truly connected with him, although I am very physically attracted. Do you think he changed? Is it possible?

Hmmm… my Magic 8 Ball says "Outlook Hazy." Even if he has changed, you would also have to undergo a major transformation to shed the betrayal and distrust you so obviously still carry. So the question is not whether he can change; the question is whether you want to risk your heart again with him. Human relationships are never certain (despite the mountains of self-help books that promise otherwise), and love is always a risk. The wisdom to remember, then, is this: Love yourself throughout the process of any risk-taking. That is, don't be so hopeful for a specific outcome, or so focused on another person or thing, that you neglect to tend to the red flags and other warning signs that alert you to an imminent avalanche.

If you look back on the relationship with this man, you will discover plenty of moments when you failed to leave or to confront his secretiveness because you feared confrontation or losing him. If you are going to return to him (or be real in any relationship), you must be willing to keep your integrity, even if it means losing your man.

Dear Joey,

I'm a therapist. I know about coping skills, I know how to grieve, but do you have any suggestions for how to let go of relationships? Four months ago the relationship that I have been in for the last two-and-a-half years ended. Within two weeks my former partner was in another relationship. I keep bumping into her and her new lover (that's the only time I see her), and they are very much in love. I want her to be happy, but it's lonely and it's hard. During this same time my best friend moved across the country. I feel like I lost my two dearest friends, and I have a hard time meeting similarly conscious people.

This is a challenging chapter of your life, so be kind to yourself. Take time to walk in nature, treat yourself to massages, and consume a diet that supports your immune system. Letting go is quite simply the process of releasing dependence on a belief. For example, if I believe, "I can't let go," it's that belief that causes pain, not the situation that I am in and use to try to prove the belief.

We use our beliefs to obstruct our ability to accept reality. But when we cling to a belief that says things should be other than the way they are, we suffer. As the sages of Zen Buddhism say, peace arrives when we accept what is.

Each time you feel lonely, it's a signal that you're not staying present for yourself. Contemporary mystic Byron Katie says, "When you're present with yourself, the whole world could fall away and you'd never notice." How can you remain present? Notice when and how you leave. For instance, do you slip away from yourself by telling yourself stories about how much happier your former partner is now? If so, practice shifting your consciousness by taking small steps toward acknowledging what you've gained by being in relationship and by being alone. Celebrate all of the ways in which your relationship with your ex-partner is complete. Remember that you and your best friend are one (as we are all one), so you can begin to see separation as the illusion that it is. Invite yourself into places where you'll meet people who share your willingness to journey into self-understanding. And give yourself all the time and support you need to heal.

Dear Joey,

I moved to town 18 months ago to be in a committed relationship, but as soon as I arrived, my boyfriend broke up with me. Recently, we started seeing each other again. We're now in a band together, making music. The problem is that our relationship lines have become blurred; we're also making love. He's going through a spiritual transformation and doesn't want a committed relationship. I'm having a hard time maintaining my sense of self. I want to be confident and be in his life, but I can't seem to do this without a commitment from him. Can you help?

Your hunger for commitment and intimacy must be satisfied, I agree, but not by this man. If you want any relationship to be elevated out of the drama of a soap opera and into the realm of holy union, you must first commit to yourself. So don't try to win him back by meeting every need or want that you suspect he may have. Instead, direct that energy into meeting your own needs and desires. In this way, you will begin to balance the relationship. Right now, your desire for a commitment from him is so big, you probably feel small and powerless. You're not. But learn how to fall in love without losing yourself. This is the path of conscious relationship. It's hard work because it begins as a solo flight when what we really want is a co-pilot. But it's worth it. And, of course, later, when we've settled comfortably into flying solo, our co-pilot often shows up.

Sex is a delicious experience with many possible consequences, but the guarantee of intimacy is not among them. In order to begin and sustain a healthy relationship with anyone else, you must commit to getting to know who you are and who you yearn to become. So either commit to yourself that you have no expectations other than enjoying sex and music with this man, or commit to each other that you will be exclusive companions consciously using the relationship as a tool for self-understanding. Since the latter requires his consent and he is unwilling, focus on the former, or bring the relationship to a close.

Dear Joey,

I'm 32 but fell in love with a 22-year-old. I don't usually date guys this young, but our relationship was wonderful. I gave more than I ever have, and he was good to me. Overnight it changed. After he dumped me, I found out he was messing with another girl. He said he wants to patch things up with me, but we see each other rarely. He has joined the Marines and will be shipped off to basic training soon. I know I love him because I can't get over him. I tried dating other men, but I miss him. I forgave him for the infidelity, but my intuition says there is more to the situation. And he doesn't love me the way I love him (he checks out other girls in front of me now). We used to sit and tell each other how special we were to one another, share our dreams and talk about our futures together. Now he treats me differently. I want things to go back to the way they were and would like your advice.

My advice? Stop living in the past. Every time you wish that your relationship would return to the way it was, you are criticizing your life as it is. That is painful. And when you deny your intuition, it also contributes to your suffering. Let me ask you a simple question and insist on only a yes or no response: Is the man you know now someone that is worthy of your heart? The only man who exists is the one you experience now. When you admit this, you will be clear about the next step to take.

I am concerned about your thought: "I know I love him because I can't get over him." Your process of grieving and healing may need more time, but this doesn't mean that you can't get over a man. It means that you would rather suffer than bring closure to the relationship that is not working. To believe that you can't get past this relationship is to impose a prison on your heart. Don't you deserve freedom?

There are other ways to interpret your experience with this man. You said that you were more giving with him than others. Perhaps the higher purpose of this relationship was to help you develop the courage to be genuine. The problem is you believe that giving of yourself should result in a man becoming a permanent fixture in your life. What if the purpose of this experience was to liberate your ability to open to a man? Don't invalidate how good and right it felt to be your open, loving self just because it didn't result in a happily-ever-after.

Dear Joey,

For 16 months I've swung between wanting to ignore my ex-girlfriend and wanting her back. She does not want me back because when I was depressed, I left angry phone messages (it temporarily relieved my sad state of mind), eventually becoming harassing. I asked for forgiveness. She granted it. But the cycle repeated. I know I need to move on, but I have contempt for her decision to date a mutual acquaintance. Sometimes when my ex says hello socially, I don't respond because I'm hurting and can't take the rejection. I'm 32 and this is my first love. I'll never give up my true feelings for this person.

Oh, honey! What are the true feelings? Animosity? Infatuation? You've had big feelings to be sure, but nothing that qualifies as love. Attachment/hate feelings are primal stuff, dating back to when you were an infant. It's best to see a qualified psychotherapist to excavate the source of this rage so that you can truly love someone in the future. Consider this: When a relationship based in genuine love ends, you still care for the former partner, and you still like her. There are no harassing phone calls. You are pleased if she is dating because you wish for her happiness. You do not present your wounds and act sullen when she says hello socially. Above all, love is patient, kind, selfless and consistent.

Dear Joey,

My girlfriend says she loves me and wants to hang out, but she cannot be my girlfriend anymore. She moved out. I loved her deeply, which is why I lived with her. She did it for financial help, not to solidify a marriage (which is where I was headed). We were friends for years before getting romantic. I never had that experience before, and it's how I knew that I loved her. I honestly thought we were going to live happily ever after. Since our breakup, we have had intimate relations. Now I've learned that she is sleeping with others. I'm going psycho over the thought of her having fun with other men. I don't want to drop a fantastic friendship over my jealousy, but I think that the only way I can shed resentment is if she is mine again, or if I write her out of my life. She says she is dating to be certain that I am "The One." I am restless and cannot let her do this in peace.

You're mourning the death of a dream: the perfect life partner and an ideal future. As you mourn, take care not to abandon yourself or God. You must trust that God is always leading you to something greater. It could be that this experience will inspire the healing of some aspect of your character. Or perhaps the sole (soul?) purpose of this relationship was to teach you how to develop a true friendship before initiating a romantic relationship. Or the closure of this relationship may be inspiration for you to trust God and yourself more deeply.

Of course, we can only trust ourselves if we are willing to tell ourselves the truth. For example, you write that you and your ex-girlfriend have had intimate relations, but she has been sleeping with other guys. I think euphemisms for sex distract us from reality. From your word choices, it appears that you initially believed that sex with you would be more meaningful to her than sex with other men. Perhaps some of your resentment results from realizing otherwise. That's a painful but vital awakening.

Here's what I think: If you're having sex with an ex-partner, the relationship is not completely broken up, but your values are. That's because, despite cultural propaganda, sex without a commitment is not love or a promise of love. It's just sex. Manipulating yourself to believe otherwise lays the foundation for self-betrayal. It also rings false that living together is preparation for marriage. A sustainable marriage is built on attraction, friendship, shared values, good communication and conflict resolution skills, trust and commitment. Those traits develop through choosing to open up to one another, not just through co-habitation. Living together works as a foundation for marriage only when the couple has already made a commitment to one another. By consciously deciding to be life partners, they don't slide into something neither is really ready for. So let yourself believe there is a woman on this planet who is waiting for your love, and move toward that dream with confidence.

Let go and let love prevail...

Be gentle with your heart. Forgive yourself for any words or behaviors that harmed the other person. Forgive yourself for the self-criticism and self-blame you lobbed against yourself. Accept full responsibility for any of the ways you contributed to the relationship's end. Unpack your resentments. Embrace the fears that lurk beneath anger and bitterness. Notice that each of these resentments lived in you long before you met your partner. Commit to cleaning out these old wounds. Otherwise, you are harming yourself. There's an old saying: Bitterness and resentment are like drinking poison and hoping someone else will get sick. Your heart deserves radiant spiritual health. Ready to let go and let love prevail? Start here:

Sit in a quiet place where you can be undisturbed by interruptions. Earplugs are helpful, but don't use an iPod. Silence is best. Close your eyes. Focus on your heart. Breathe into your heart. Notice how that feels. Keep breathing until your heart and the space around it relaxes.

Ask yourself for three words to describe what you really want now from your former partner. For example: compassion, friendship, an apology.

As you inhale, say the first word. As you exhale, repeat that word. Do this for each word. As you breathe, notice all the ways you already have each quality in your life: How do you express compassion? How have others offered compassion to you? Name the ways that you befriend yourself. Apologize to yourself, saying to yourself what you wish your partner would say.

Acknowledge that you cannot hold your former partner responsible for healing you. Accept that only you have the power to transform yourself. For your sake, accept that you have what you really need. Refuse to believe your mind as it tries to seduce you into believing that you are not enough or that you lack something that only your partner can give you.

Resentment is an attempt to remain in the past. It stunts our spiritual health and keeps us too small to create lives of full contribution and meaning. So forgive, let go, breathe into your greatness. If you failed to address problems because you feared your partner would respond poorly or even leave, admit it. If you ignored your intuition about infidelity or other betrayals because you wanted a relationship more than you wanted the truth, acknowledge that to yourself. Forgive your former partner for whatever you perceive she or he did. Forgiveness does not mean that nothing happened. Forgiveness is letting go of allowing someone else to have more power over your happiness and health than you do. Forgiveness is also wide with a compassion born of the understanding that each of us has, consciously or unconsciously, hurt others at some point. We forgive for our own sake. Forgiveness returns us to the real work of life: giving and receiving love.

Acknowledgements...

"Gratitude is the heart's first language." — Joey Garcia

I am grateful to have transcended my heartbreaks through nurturing by dear friends and healers. Each lovingly challenged me to grow and encouraged me to publicly share the insights gained on my journey. Jan Haag has been an endlessly generous guide, champion and true friend. Melinda Welsh trusted me to write an advice column for the readers of The Sacramento News & Review, transforming my life forever. Michael Nelson, J.C. Allen and Tim Foley have always listened to my life stories and inspired me to reach higher and further than I imagined possible. Claire Collingwood reminded me to let go and move forward. Jane Anne Staw believed in me as a writer, and still does. Linda Tidgewell, Byron Katie, Janice Farrell and Bill Blazek are spiritual teachers with truly priceless wisdom. Your love informs my life. Laura Martin believed in this project, structured it, kept it alive, and created its beautiful design. And Kathy Carlisle, bright light and kick-ass creative partner-in-crime: thank you, thank you, thank you.

About the author...

Joey Garcia has listened to thousands of stories of heartbreak as a life strategy consultant, radio personality and, since 1996, as an advice columnist for the Sacramento News & Review. She ably guides adults and adolescents into the freedom and happiness that comes from understanding how to transform suffering into wisdom. Joey's passion for service and her creative perspective on living fully is an inspiration for all who seek to fulfill their potential. Enjoy the free resources at **www.JoeyGarcia.com,** including Joey's blog. You can also order the following products:

How to Date like an Adult (2014)

52 Ways to Love meditation cards

Love Lessons CD series

Joey is the founder of Rise Up Belize! a 501(c)(3) that offers free summer camps and high school scholarships for children in Belize, Central America, and free professional development training for Belizean primary school teachers. You can join her in supporting social justice at *www.riseupbelize.org*.

25453569R20074

Made in the USA
Charleston, SC
02 January 2014